Samuel Beckett Is Closed

Samuel Beckett Is Closed

Michael Coffey

FOXROCK BOOKS, NEW YORK

Published by Foxrock Books/Evergreen Review in association with
OR Books/Counterpoint Press.
Distributed to the trade by Publishers Group West.

Visit our website at evergreenreview.com.

First printing 2018.

Library of Congress Cataloging-in-Publication Data:
A catalog record for this book is available from the Library of Congress.

British Library Cataloging in Publication Data:
A catalog record for this book is available from the British Library.

Text and jacket design and typesetting by Laura Lindgren.
Set in Carre Noir, Century 731, CA Cula, Magma, and Sofia.

Printed by Berryville Graphics, Virginia.

hardback ISBN 978-1-944869-59-5 · ebook ISBN 978-1-944869-54-0

Excerpts from Samuel Beckett's *Long Observation of the Ray* © The Estate
of Samuel Beckett. Reproduced by kind permission of the Estate of Samuel
Beckett c/o Rosica Colin Limited, London (p. 120). The torture scenarios are
adapted from Mohamedou Ould Slahi's *Guantanamo Diary*, edited by Larry
Siems, Little, Brown, 2015. The torture investigation procedures are taken
from *The US Army Field Manual on Interrogation 34—52*, and the investigation
into detainee treatment is based on the Schmidt-Furlow investigation, under
the auspices of the Senate Armed Service Committee's "Inquiry into the
Treatment of Detainees in U.S. Custody." Reports of terrorist attacks in Paris
are adapted from Google-translated Agence France Press reports at the time.

"Being is constantly putting form in danger."
—Samuel Beckett

"B: Total object, complete with missing parts, instead of partial object. Question of degree.

"D: More. The tyranny of the discreet overthrown. The world a flux of movements partaking of living time, that of effort, creation, liberation. . . . The fleeting instant of sensation given back, given forth, with context of the continuum it nourished."
—Samuel Beckett and Georges Duthuit, from *Three Dialogues*

PART ONE

I.

—It's not cricket, Sam.

I've spent the last three years reading only the writings of Samuel Beckett.

Tell me a story, she says—*that*'ll put me to sleep.

The detention and interrogation operation covered a three-year period and over 24,000 interrogations.

—So we *won't* be here for five days. The prospect of *nine* innings gave me a fright. We'd be panting here through August.

I exaggerate a little: I have read newspapers and the books of friends and a few literary journals, but I've not wandered in search of other major writers to discover or reread. I have read (and reread) only Beckett (and books about his work), while also becoming a member of the Samuel Beckett Society, subscribing to the *Journal of Beckett Studies* out of Edinburgh University, attending a Beckett conference, in Phoenix, and visiting the Beckett Collection at the University of Reading in England, then Antwerp, with Halifax next, as the Beckett conferences roll on.

I can confirm that my stories *do* put her to sleep, on those occasions when I am stirred to render an old account or, as happens more often of late, am summoned by my beloved to perform. This power—to put people down, to take them under, to usher them from this side of the veil to the other—Christ, I'm nodding out myself. What I mean to say is this—that it is my voice simply that serves as a calmative.

> This investigation found only three interrogation acts in violation of techniques authorized by the Army Field Manual and Department of Defense. The report found that the interrogation of a high-value detainee resulted in degrading and abusive treatment but did not rise to the level of being inhuman. The report found no evidence of torture.

—I will. That's our man there? A crisp ale would do me, in this heat.

—Afraid the best we've got here is Rheingold, [*singing*] *the dry beer.* They sponsor this spectacle.

—I'd drink bog water from a galosh right now.

—Two over here!

> I am sixty-two years old. How many years of reading do I have left? Let's say twenty, which is a little optimistic but not unreasonable. I'm healthy. Let's assume so. My eyes are good.

I mix them up, the rhythms of my speech, all my cadences, of which I have a few—fast or slow, chipper or lugubrious, and the accents as well—my old rural honk or the Irish brogue, for the poetry. And then there's the timbre, and the register, and that subtle interplay of adduction and abduction—I am talking open and shut here. Puffs of air. It is certainly not the content of my stories that induces unconsciousness, or so I tell myself, for I must—*in order to live with the choices I have made!* Which is to say, were I in fact capable of delivering pure device-agnostic content that could alter states of being, I should have found a different career, hiring myself out to surgeries and day-care centers, say, where putting people under is to be wished, and then making my texts available (for a subscription) for others to intone. There I go again, nearly comatose.

> *You have been identified as having conducted an assignment at GTMO, Cuba, since 9/11/2001. The Inspection Division has been tasked with contacting those employees who have served in any capacity at GTMO. Employees should immediately respond to the following: If you observed aggressive treatment, which was not consistent with guidelines, respond via email for purposes of follow-up interview; if you observed no aggressive treatment of detainees you should respond documenting a negative response. The above email was sent to 493 FBI personnel who had served at GTMO.*

—Were they in town, I'd have taken you to see the first-place Yanks.

—Now why is that?

—To see a little professionalism, and the great Mickey Mantle.

—These are . . . amateurs then?

—Virtually . . . and retirees.

—Pensioners—the pure game, for the love of it. Nothing like it. [*Grandly, as if quoting*] The presence of promise is a curse. [*Snidely*] Thanks, Mother. *Maa.*

At this age, I know who it is I want to read—though, really, have I read all of Shakespeare or Dickens or (any of) Balzac? Should I? I have not read the bulk of Proust even—*prochaine, prochaine.* So it is Beckett. I just don't know why. The dedicated Beckett reading began as I waited out the publication of my first book of stories. These stories were much about identity and adoption and fathers and heirs both literary and otherwise and I did not know what the book's reception would tell me about myself—I would have to wait and see. I sometimes think I don't like waiting but the opposite is true—I find waiting for something inherently exciting—and waiting for a book to be published is particularly exquisite; I even find waiting for something miserable, like, say, a colonoscopy, a luxury, as every day that is not the dreaded day has a certain satin lining. Even so, during such an interim as prepublication represents, I was concerned about having a focus to my activities.

It's a funny thing—at least I pretend to laugh at it—that she cannot sleep these days. I don't mean that she *never* sleeps, for she does, and not only with the aid of my soporifics. She can sleep perfectly well and on her own in boxcars rolling over land and in the theater houses of an afternoon, or at the back of the slow taverns we frequent when we are flush, availing ourselves of the steam-table fare and the Four Roses. Oh, will she sleep! But come time for the bedsheets or the pallet or the rug, I mean night-night, in our kip, she's as jumpy as a puppet on a string. Where'd that come from? Rhymes with spring, now I remember. One of my tropes, spring is, funny how that happens in these little canters.

The investigating officer was directed to address the following allegations:

- That military interrogators improperly used military working dogs to threaten detainees.
- That military interrogators improperly used duct tape to cover a detainee's mouth and head.
- That Department interrogators improperly impersonated agents and other Department officers during the interrogation of detainees.
- That on several occasions Department interrogators improperly played loud music and yelled loudly at detainees
- That military interrogators improperly used sleep deprivation against detainees.
- That military interrogators improperly chained detainees and placed them in a fetal position on the floor.

> - That military interrogators improperly used extremes
> of heat and cold during their interrogation of
> detainees.

—The men in blue suits and the little caps, what do they do?

　—They enforce the rules.

　—We'll stay on their good side, so.

　—Both these teams are new, only two years old. The league added them—expansion, they called it— and the rosters are a few kids and a lot of has-beens. Frankly, Sam, they're pitiful.

　—Oh, excellent! Stir in a little fear and we'll have catharsis.

　—That's what I think, too, to be honest. You have the makings of a Mets fan, Sam. I'm going to get you a cap. For the sun.

　—For the shade.

As I woke up each day anticipating an eventual book launch, and readings and a party and, god willing, reviews, I didn't want to make it up each day, my reading that is. I wanted to have decided that already, to have had it decided. One of the things I learned in writing my short fiction was to interrogate what a given story is about. This often helped me shape it—or abandon it. So as I plunged into my Beckett reading two summers ago, rereading James Knowlson's biography, and Beckett's early stories, and a book about the diaries he kept while in Germany in the late 1930s, I asked myself this question: Why Beckett? In the ensuing months I have chased that ball, let me tell you. For example, I was convinced I had discovered that Beckett was the father of an American writer, which promised to be a shocking revelation, not only to those who understand Beckett as having such insight into life's lack of meaning that he would never bring another being into it—"They give birth astride of a grave, the light gleams an instant, then it's night," says Pozzo in *Godot*—but a shock as well to the Beckett estate: a sole "heir of the body?" I became transfixed by the work of this American writer, little known broadly but admired and respected by a certain avant-garde, here and in Europe. Her work is marked by a deep engagement with a purely American—indeed New England tradition of puritanism filtered through a metaphysics of writing, feminism, and the spiritual extremism of a historic poetics convinced of God's Immanence. This seemed to me not the polar opposite of Samuel Beckett's inherited tradition and his rebellions, but a crafted dissent. This is not me, her work declared. I am not my father's daughter. Not *that* father. I have another.

To put her under as she thrashes about the bedsheets or upon the pallet or the rug, depending on our whereabouts and our fortunes, I often embark upon a verbal tour of the seasons. If you are not convinced by now that it is not my content that has the magic but my delivery, then ponder how it is that my most reliable oratory invokes the cycle of the seasons, either the condensed version or one of the four, in turn, in full, spring to summer to fall to winter. I mean, how dull that is. Basically, I am talking about the weather and yet, the power! You should see it. Magic potion, my words are. If she is not out cold by the time I get to winter then it is not me but another chap who has slipped into the bedchamber with her, as has happened, but we are beyond that—that was Toledo. By the vernal equinox, my otherwise jumpy puppet can be found so shallowly breathing as to seem dead, and she has never made it conscious to my rendition of Opening Day, which is a pity as it is one of my most vivid re-creations, complete with the rural accents and a few clever sound effects, crack of the bat and such. Shall I? Yes, spring, for old time's sake. Perhaps for a little practice, a little boning up? *Tenez-vous bien.*

> The investigators were ordered to investigate two additional allegations concerning a female military interrogator performing a "lap dance" on a detainee and the use of faux "menstrual blood" during an interrogation. The investigators were told furthermore not to limit themselves to the listed allegations. The investigating team attempted to determine if the allegations in fact occurred. During the course of the follow-up investigation, allegations raised specifically by the two detainees who were subjects of the first and second "Special Interrogation Plans," respectively, were considered. The investigating team applied a preponderance standard of proof consistent with the guidelines provided to determine if a particular interrogation approach fell properly within an authorized technique. In those cases in which the team concluded

that the allegation had in fact occurred, the team then considered whether the incident was in compliance with techniques approved either at the time of the incident or subsequent to the incident. In those cases where it was determined the allegation had occurred and to have not been an authorized technique, the team then reviewed whether disciplinary action had already been taken and the propriety of that action. The team did not review the legal validity of the various interrogation techniques in question. **Background**: Interrogation operations began in January. Initially, interrogators relied upon interrogation techniques contained in FM 34-52. These techniques were ineffective. In October, the Commander requested approval of nineteen counter-resistance techniques, broken down into three categories, the third being the most aggressive. The Secretary approved categories 1 and 2 but only one of the techniques in category 3 was authorized—non-injurious physical contact.

—There's a stroke!

　—That should be caught . . . attaboy!

　—Now they change innings?

　—Now the home team hits, if you want to call it that. You finished your beer? What's the verdict?

　—*Bouquet des champignons.*

　—That bad?

　—I'll get these.

There is no dispute about Beckett having had an affair with the American writer's mother in the late summer of 1936, a Dublin woman with whom Beckett had grown up in Foxrock. The families knew each other well. The woman, in 1936, was already married to an American legal scholar—she had just returned to Dublin as chaperone for two unmarried Boston ladies in the style of the day. But Beckett's family, wary of a scandal, urged the end to the liaison. Beckett fled to Germany—as he had done before when under duress—and the woman returned to Boston. The daughter was born nine months later. She looks like Beckett. She affects a Beckett look, to this day—short cropped gray hair; she is possessed of the aquiline nose and what look like Beckett's gnarled fingers, possibly from Dupuytren's contracture, sometimes known as "the Celtic hand." Her literary style is austere, her aesthetic uncompromising, a kind of literary abstraction.

Such springs as I recall them begin with a sense of a cool damp emanating from the ground, just thawing, all kinds of dead matter giving up their odors, to us, fair children, out to play. The color and cold of promise! Then the buds dotting the tree branches like a hesitant code or speech, on the way to another form, a blossoming, into birds and then the damn bees. Oh, the bees that zither through the air in their dizzy loops, almost making fun of menace, so harmless, so necessary, don't sting me. I can go on, to digging up the bait from the earth warmed by the burn barrel, with my Gramps, whose old heavy boot would thump the spade in but slowly, slowly and then as slowly turn over a loaf of earth, enlivened by the wriggling heads, or tails—there is no difference, to me—of garden worms. He would then gently chunk the hunk apart, in sections, revealing long annelid strands, purple and gray, and these would go into this disused tobacco can with handfuls of dirt and bits of grass, and then we'd give the trout hell in the stream. I would seldom, if at all, in my telling, go into the details of impaling these creatures on a barbed Eagle number 9, and resolutely never extend to describing the actual tricking of a trout to lurch at the dangling meal with the fatal business concealed within, for this was narrative information of a tenor that might agitate rather than sedate my lovely.

The Secretary issued a new policy accepting twenty-four techniques. The Secretary's guidance remains in effect today. First, it required all detainees to continue to be treated humanely. Second, it required notification prior to the implementation of the following aggressive interrogation techniques: Incentive/Removal of Incentive, Pride and Ego Down, Mutt and Jeff, and Isolation. Third, it specifically limited the use of these aggressive techniques to circumstances required by "military necessity." The memorandum did not attempt to define the parameters of "humane treatment" or "military necessity." Mutt and Jeff are the stars of a comic strip that began in 1908. They are stupid and scheming risk-takers, horse players, gamblers, one more stupid than the other.

—This is what you would call the home side. Look!
    —He keeps running?
    —Around the bases, that diamond, really a square—first base, second, third, home—if he can. Bobby Klaus—slides into second!

Beckett sent a gift when she was born. He sent it to America. Most scholars I have spoken to off the record say the math doesn't work—more than nine months between the mother's return by boat to Boston and the birth of the daughter. I tired of doing the math, which proved no such thing—parturition is forty weeks, not nine months, for starters. The math doesn't rule anything out—or in. But a DNA test does, proving that the writer is not Beckett's daughter but the daughter of the legal scholar and her mother, a relief, no doubt, for her mother, too, was unsure, and often tormented her young daughter and then not-so-young daughter that indeed she might be a Beckett.

She would even call for it. In the dark I would hear a mewing, unmistakably hers, mewing to me, *give me a story* was the translation, *tell me a story, put me away*. And I would, happily. To be asked for a tale, a rendition, with a decided purpose, as if asked for a tool, *bring me the hammer, love*, it was so pleasing. Of course, I will, dear. And to see her drop under in but a short while kept me in awe of the powers, not my own, but of language itself, and our human voice, something comes from somewhere shaping something that then is consumed, in these instances like a narcotic or a draught . . . what can it be but literature!

Allegation: That Department interrogators improperly impersonated agents or other Department officers during the interrogation session. **Finding**: On several occasions, various Department interrogators impersonated agents and other Department officers. **Technique**: Authorized technique of Deceiving Interrogator Identity. **Discussion**: The interrogation chief agreed to stop the practice of impersonation. The Senior Supervisory Agent was pleased with the Chief's rapid and thorough response.

—Look! Play at home. . . . He's out!

> As an adoptee myself, having wondered about my origins, who my parents were, for fifty years, and trying to figure this out while pursuing writing, I felt for this American writer. I was deeply curious about how this affected her practice. But I dropped it.

One spring, it was spring cleaning, nothing but industry around my domicile, the one in which I lived in my early years, by the grace of some strange relations, perhaps my parents, I was never sure, only of Gramps I was sure, that's what he told me, when I could understand such things, to call him. He and the others, there were two or three others, he was the oldest, I can hazard that without fear of contradiction, would busy about the brooms and mops and buckets and all manner of chemistry after the long winter of holing up indoors, beyond the blizzards.

> *An interrogator must not pass himself off as a medic, man of god, or member of the Red Cross. To every technique, there are hundreds of possible variations, each of which can be developed for a specific situation or source. The variations are limited only by the interrogator's personality, experience, ingenuity, and imagination.*

—We remain at love, then?

I thought, that's not "Why Beckett"—it is her story, not mine.

The rooms were aired.

Much of the information of value to the interrogator is information the source is not aware he has.

II.

—Where's Coffey?

I first heard of Samuel Beckett when I was a
teenager living in a small town in upstate New York.

My job was to stay out of the way, a skill I found easy to
master.

An individual's value system is easier to bypass
immediately after undergoing traumatic experience.

—Ah, Joe Coffey had to go. He's watching Sidney do
the final scrub-up edits.
—Joe did a nice job, once we got through the
street scene and that bockety trolley.

The world beyond, such as we understood the
concept, came to us through the network evening
news. I figure, in retrospect, that it was the fall of
1969, when Beckett's play *Breath* had its premiere
in the UK. It made the end of the half-hour newscast
as a curiosity, as something outrageous and, I
thought, it might just be fun.

I would busy myself about the grounds, picking up branches and dead leaves and old bread bags and beer cans with their little drivel of honey-colored liquid inside. On one occasion, feeling particularly diligent, the day getting a little warm for my tastes, I decided to explore beneath the porch, the narrow space, dark and all dirt, a place that never saw the sun, where nothing grew. It was rank.

> **Allegation**: That a female military interrogator performed a "lap dance" on a detainee during an interrogation.
> **Finding**: On one occasion between October and January a female interrogator put perfume on a detainee by touching the detainee on his arm with her hand.
> **Technique**: Authorized, as mild, non-injurious physical touching.

—Cutting that opening shot was key. Alan was distraught, Boris was a wreck, Joe was in a misery, for him, the damn thing was so fucked, *pardon*. We were all surprised at your fix.

—My greatest contribution, I guess: *"Cut!"* Eisenstein doesn't know what he missed.

> The anchor, or news reader, was Walter Cronkite, by then famously war- and assassination-wearied. Near the end of his broadcast, he presented news of a play by an Irish playwright that, from curtain to curtain, lasted half a minute, nothing but a pile of junk on stage, a cry, and one inspiration of breath, and one breath out. The theater patrons were angry, said Uncle Walter. The playwright had won the Nobel Prize the year before, so they expected

an exalted night at the theater, not a short glimpse of rubble. The world and beyond was coming apart, this seemed clear to Walter Cronkite. He said, "And that's the way it is," at which he arched his eyebrows a bit, which said to me, "C'mon, people, we've seen worse."

I peered across the expanse of the understory, might I say eight by eighteen feet or so, for it was a nice porch, the finest feature of the house, on which rockers rocked and the newspaper was left by the boy every morning. I was sure that things, light things, paper and leaves, had blown in beneath the porch, and they should be fetched and disposed of just as those out in the open, should they not? I took my own counsel and decided yes, they should, Gramps would approve. So down I went, on all fours, and then to a belly crawl, like a soldier advancing beneath enemy wire. The dark was complete or would have been complete but for the dim light around the borders, allowing one, that is, me, to dimly make out objects.

Finding: During the month of March a female interrogator approached a detainee from behind, rubbed against his back, leaned and touched him on his knee and then shoulder and whispered in his ear that his situation was futile, and she ran her fingers through his hair. Technique: Authorized, act used to highlight futility of the detainee's situation. Discussion: Chief stated that he specifically directed the interrogator to go to the PX and purchase rose oil with the intent of rubbing a portion of the perfume on the detainee's arm to distract him. The interrogator admitted to using this approach. At the time of the event the detainee responded by attempting to bite the interrogator, lost his balance, fell out of his chair, and broke a tooth. **Organizational response**: The interrogator was not disciplined for rubbing perfume on the detainee since this was an authorized technique.

—An inning with no runs. Marvelous stuff. And here's another go.

—More of the same, likely. Though I will tell you that the Houston pitcher, back in '56, did something no one else has ever done or will ever do in the history of the game.

—That bad?

—Not at all: he threw a perfect game, and *in a World Series*, our championship series, the equivalent of. . . . The Ashes. He was a Yankee then. Woke up with a hangover and then went out and let no batter get on base, with everything on the line, twenty-seven straight outs. Hadn't happened in thirty years.

—So this man's a great drinker. *And* a great bowler?

In 1974, I got away from the Catholic university I was attending in order to spend my junior year abroad studying Irish literature and history in Dublin. Beckett—and Joyce and Yeats—were colossal figures in dirty old Dublin, and we all had our work cut out for us—none of us had any idea of the dramatic and very public career of Yeats the poet, or of the magnificence of *Ulysses* and *Portrait* and *Dubliners*, or of the mystifying Beckett, still alive and living in Paris. We read his first novel, *Murphy*, his collection of stories, and the imposing trilogy—or, as Beckett preferred them to be called, Three Novels. *Murphy* and the book of stories weren't sold to us as great literature; and the three novels were more of a curiosity, as far as I could tell. The Irish seemed more enamored of Flann O'Brien than Samuel Beckett at that time. We students were encouraged to take our measure of the Irish literary tradition in and about Dublin—we visited the Martello Tower, Sandymount Strand, Davy Byrne's Pub, and 7 Eccles Street, all sites in *Ulysses*. There were Yeats plays on at any given time in our stay, and we saw several, all fairly awful—but there were no Beckett plays. However, in the common room at the school I attended there was a hi-fi and several "Irish" records—the Chieftains, the great tenor John McCormack, and a Caedmon recording of an actor named Jack MacGowran reading Beckett texts.

Indeed, in the dark beneath the porch, a few cans and what looked to be a half-bale of advertising circulars, crumpled and huddled together, loomed into view. And then a kind of gray lump with a stick rising above it, till it disappeared, the stick did, into the studs holding the porch flooring together. I advanced. Imagine the alarm of recognizing the neighbor's cat or what looked like the neighbor's cat, Tom. I fled but only inside myself. My mind, or what I consider such, recoiled back down the length of me to the soles of my feet but I did not move.

Then my mind bobbed up again, to the surface, to the front of me, having left in its path a knotted stomach. I decided to make a noise, to wake old Tom. But Tom was dusty, Tom did not stir, Tom was not asleep or hiding, the stick was his tail.

> **Allegation**: That a female military interrogator wiped "menstrual blood" on a detainee during an interrogation. **Finding**: In March a female interrogator told a detainee that red ink on her hand was menstrual blood and then put her hand on the detainee's arm. **Technique**: Authorized, act used to highlight the futility of the detainee's situation. **Discussion**: The female interrogator is no longer in military service and has declined to be interviewed. According to the Chief's deputy, the incident occurred when a detainee spat in the interrogator's face. According to the Chief's deputy, the interrogator left the room crying. She developed a plan to psychologically get back at him. She touched the detainee on his shoulder, showed him the red ink on her hand and said she was menstruating. The detainee threw himself on the floor and started banging his head.

—A champion drinker, they say, but really a rather average pitcher . . . bowler . . . except for that one day. He was *king*.

—And the deaf may hear and the dumb may speak. Plenty of hope . . . if not for us. Good Kafka . . .

—This kid here's a local boy, the one batting, Kranepool. When I said kids I meant him. He came up at seventeen. There's a blast!

—Now there, Dick. It's just the long out. He

doesn't look like an athlete. A golfer maybe, a duffer you'd see wading the dimples at Carrickmines.

> I can still recall MacGowran's richly comic Irish accent, and the way he dove through texts that looked banal on the page and made them funny, sad, vital. "I shall soon be quite dead at last in spite of all. Perhaps next month. Then it will be the month of April or of May. For the year is still young, a thousand little signs tell me so. Perhaps I am wrong, perhaps I shall survive Saint John the Baptist's Day and even the Fourteenth of July, festival of freedom. Indeed I would not put it past me to pant on to the Transfiguration . . . " The scorn in MacGowran's voice in "festival of freedom" and the impatience with the character's likely persistence in hanging on was shocking to me, yet I found myself laughing. At least, when I left Dublin, if I had not seen a Beckett play, I had his voice. The voice he liked, at least one anyway, was that of Jack MacGowran, whom Beckett would help until the hard-drinking actor's death, in New York, at age fifty-four, assistance that was extended to MacGowran's widow. "Happy to waive performance royalties anytime and anywhere for the benefit of Jackie's Gloria," Beckett wrote.

I touched his side, old Tom, where I used to rub him. He was hard as a suitcase. I reversed field. I found Gramps and told him there was a dead cat under the porch. He looked at me with pity and told me to fetch him the rake and a burlap bag. I didn't say "Tom." It wasn't Tom. She used to like that story. Oh, we were young then—the more detail, the better. Tom was dusty, yes. Hard as a suitcase, yes. Use the language, go ahead, use it all up.

> **Allegation**: The interrogators improperly played loud music and yelled loudly at detainees. **Finding**: On numerous occasions, detainees were yelled at or subjected to loud music during interrogation. **Technique**: Authorized—Incentive and Futility—acts used as reward for cooperating or to create futility of not cooperating. **Discussion**: On a few occasions detainees were left alone in the interrogation booth for an indefinite period of time while loud music played and strobe lights flashed. The vast majority of yelling and music was accomplished with interrogators in the room. The volume was never loud enough to cause any physical injury. Futility technique included the playing of loud electric guitar and the reciting of doggerel over a monotonous beat. **Organization response**: None. **Recommendation**: The allegation should be closed. Recommend the development of specific guidance on the length of time that a detainee may be subjected to futility music.

—These are excellent seats, Dick. I must thank you.

—Judith did it. Barney didn't have a clue, but Judith can get anything off anyone.

—I'll attest to the persuasions of Miss Schmidt. She *is* Grove Press, no offense.

—I'll tell her.

—You can admire the geometry of the game from here, that diamond shape, as you call it, its outer boundaries there in white lime is it, or chalk, and the blue wall closing it all in. The game has a spatial beauty, in its proportions. But if we were over there [*pointing far to his right*] that geometry would collapse, visually. It would look like a runway.

> The three novels: I remember thinking they were all one novel, I thought they talked about each other, but I swear that this was not an approved way of looking at *Molloy*, *Malone Dies*, and *The Unnamable* at that time (though now it is). There was no biography yet. Beckett was lumped in with existentialists—with Sartre, Ionesco. I read more about an obscure Flemish philosopher named Geulincx, not knowing quite why, and boned up on Dante, not his *Inferno* or *Paradiso* but *Purgatorio*, because Beckett favored a character there named Belacqua, a paragon of indolence who enjoyed the fetal position at all times, preferably in the lee of a boulder. Dante was fond of Belacqua also. Back at my Catholic university for my senior year, an acting company from San Quentin came to campus and put on Beckett's *Endgame*. A guy doing life played Hamm. The audience coughed throughout the performance. Our professor said to us after, over schooners of beer in a nearby pub, it was "manifestations of discomfort" in the crowd. I found the play hilarious—even if it was about the end of the world.

There's a power to story and words, the old tenor and vehicle, don't let me belittle that notion. At a memorial for my beloved's mother, where the departure of a real being is marked by memories brought forth by the invited and the sponsors, a simple song was sung, beautifully, so beautifully, in a fine Fifth Avenue church on a fine spring morning or afternoon, I don't recall, but in daylight, sure it was. And the singer sang some song, swaying up there where the pulpit stood useless and barren. She sang, "Was it real? Was it real? Was it real? Yes it was, yes it was, yes it was." Don't know why that rips at me so, tears came, come. I shared this with my beloved, though the tale is not fit for service as nocturnal narcotic, but only in the daylight, over sweet rolls, once, on a special day, and at other times over the cracker, many times over the cracker. It was a nice memory, my crying, for me, and the sentiment. I was fond of it. For if it was real, whatever *it* is and whatever *was* means and whatever *real* is, and if you can ask it that question and affirm that yes, *it was so*, then it's a life. And that's what a memorial is all about—an afterlife in expression.

> **Allegation**: That military interrogators improperly used extremes of heat and cold during their interrogation of detainees. **Finding**: On several occasions during 2002 and 2003 interrogators would adjust the air conditioner to make the detainee uncomfortable. **Technique**: Authorized, per Secretary Memorandum. **Discussion**: Many interrogators believed the detainee's comfort in the hot climate of his homeland caused a differing in opinions regarding the use of air conditioning units in the interrogation booths. They stuffed ice cubes in his shirt.

The camp was locked down the whole day. Around 10 p.m. I was pulled out of my cell and taken to the X building. The room was extremely cold.

—Once a stage manager . . .

—I did learn that much, I learned a lot from Alan Schneider. It's a problem. For which perspective are we staging the play, I asked. He said that was his job, mine was *from* which perspective. Well I'm helpless there—let's put another leaf on the tree, now let's take it off—that sort of thing.

At the Beckett Conference in Phoenix, I heard a paper delivered on Beckett's *Texts for Nothing*, thirteen beautiful prose pieces composed in the early 1950s, as Beckett wound down from the brutal but brilliant period of postwar creativity, a "frenzy of writing," one biographer called it, in which Beckett wrote his most famous works—*Godot*, *Endgame*, and the novels *Molloy*, *Malone Dies*, and *The Unnamable*. What caught my attention in this paper was that the habitually self-derogating Beckett actually liked these pieces. "Some of the little *Textes pour rien* of 1951 are all right I think," he wrote in a letter to a friend. He said in another letter, "They are worth publishing."

Ghosts are real, by which I mean they are real people. They have distinct voices, like real people do. You can hear them. They have a presence. You can see them, and feel them, and smell them, decked out in their unique fashion, whether sackcloth or linen or leisure wear, their voices modulated by their physiques. They can crop up anywhere. My father, I can hear him now, can hear his silence in this particular moment, looking from afar, inviting me in, interested, interested, such is love.

I was just shaking. I made up my mind not to argue anymore with the interrogators. I'm just going to sit there like a stone, and let them do the talking. Many detainees decided to do so. They were taken day after day to interrogation in order to break them. I am sure some got broken because nobody can bear agony the rest of his life.

—There's a lot of futility in this game. These lads cannot defend their wicket, as we say, *at all*. And they can barely get the ball out of the pitch when they do make a strike.

I came to love these *Texts for Nothing* pieces so much that I read them over and over and convinced myself that I was a quite superior reader. As I read them, silently to myself, they sounded like poetry, comedy, philosophy. I looked around for audio recordings of these beauties. But there was only a little of Jack MacGowran—just a portion of one of the thirteen pieces—and some performances by Bill Irwin that, alas, went unrecorded.

Dad's quiet today, as always, then he's not. Listen to the light, now, I hear. You've always loved light.

The team decided to take me back to the cold room. Maybe it wasn't so cold for somebody wearing regular shoes, underwear, and a jacket like the interrogators, but

*it was definitely cold for a detainee with flip-flops and no
underwear. "Talk to us!" XXXX shouted.*

—It's the Mets, Sam.

I was on my own.

This one room.

"I am ready to cooperate unconditionally," I told him.

III.

–Perhaps no runs will be made, then what?

> I decided I would record all thirteen of the *Texts for Nothing* and put the audio files on the Internet.

I love you, Father.

> **Allegation**: That military interrogators improperly used sleep deprivation against detainees.

—We can't presume anything. They played for ten hours last month. One game went twenty-three innings.

> Let the Beckett Estate come after me for copyright violation. But I was stymied by the very first text, which begins, "Suddenly, no, at last, long last." I couldn't convincingly render that reversal, almost a deletion, despite many takes—how to negate one utterance with another within six words and then carry on believably?

Then Father says, *Why?* For fuck's sake, did he really? Ghosts are like that, lurking at the margins, in dreams, in the silence beneath overheard conversations, and then, as in a dream and often in a dream, you get delivery of a query: it shows they have been watching, and we call it caring.

> **Finding**: Some detainees were subjected to cell moves every few hours to disrupt sleep patterns and lower the ability to resist interrogation. Each case differed as to length and frequency of cell moves. **Technique**: Neither sleep disruption or deprivation is an authorized FM 34–52 technique.

—It's charming, in its way. The struggle. Trudging back to their bench trailing the bat. Something grand about it. The crowd is enjoying it, or am I wrong?

   —They are connoisseurs of losing, Sam.

   —An acquired taste.

> I tried Text 3: "Leave, I was going to say leave all that. What matter who's speaking, someone said what matter who's speaking. There's going to be a departure . . . " What emphasis or intonation to put on the first "leave?" I was over my head. Text 4: "I'll describe the place," writes Beckett, and then, "that's unimportant."

Because you brought me to ball games, I say. Because you told me about Louis-Schmeling. Let's remember Louis-Schmeling, my father. Tell me about tuning in to the fight on a summer's night on the blighted farm during the Depression, you were a boy, hating farming, wanting somewhere else, something else, excited about the world's conflicts, there was importance in the air, there was Roosevelt cheering us on ("We need your muscles, Joe, against Germany")—and here you were rooting for Joe, a negro from the South with two stones for hands to pummel a Nazi to death, as he said he wished to. And you wished it, too. Tell me again, Father, about your mix of disappointment and thrill when the fight ended in two minutes, the German squealing on the canvas, the stadium roaring, the nation roaring, you could hear it all on the radio, McCarthy was it calling the blows—some Irishman. I loved that, Father, you were but a boy.

Technique: The exact parameters of sleep deprivation technique remained undefined until Commander established clear guidance on the use of sleep adjustment. With the Commander's guidance, sixteen-hour interrogations were repeated in a twenty-hour cycle, not to exceed four days in succession.

For the next seventy days I wouldn't know the sweetness of sleeping: interrogation twenty-four hours a day, three and sometimes four shifts a day. "If you start to cooperate you'll have some sleep and hot meals," they used to tell me repeatedly.

Recommendation: No disciplinary action is required. The allegation should be closed.

—I certainly will not have another right now, thank you. I'd nod.
—You'd miss nothing.
—Will no one win? What then?

—They play to the end. Timeless, this sport. No clock.

—No one losing would be an excellent terminus—a draw, as it were. Scoreless even a better draw.

> I happen to think place is most important, not that Beckett doesn't—he goes on in Text 4 to give an "unimportant" description of "place," but he gives it: "The top, very flat, of a mountain, no, a hill, but so wild so wild." Enough. He adds "Enough." But it is not nearly enough for me, per usual. Beckett was either all inflection or no inflection. He was either theater or mathematics. I laughed at myself and my little iPhone audio files and deleted them—there's a reversal for you. I had before me the cut pages of my Calder and Boyars edition of *Texts for Nothing*. I had arrayed the pages on the floor so as to not to have to hear on the recording the sound of my amateurish turning of those pages: a waste.

You gave me the word once, Father. You were gone, but I was alone and scared. I was in some county the name of which you would know and I would not. I was on my own, driving in a car south of the Hall of Fame, where we had visited when I was but a Little Leaguer, and you had shown me the exhibit, earnestly, all the exhibits, bats and balls and gloves in some magical town devoted to a pastime. But was it past? I had gone there again. You know I bought an umbrella? Why does anyone buy an umbrella? For protection!

> In 1992, Mohamedou Ould Slahi, a twenty-two-year-old Mauritanian, was completing his degree in electrical

engineering at the University of Duisberg, Germany. He was living there with his Mauritanian wife. In 1992, the US Department of the Army issued Field Manual 34-52 on Intelligence Interrogation, a 177-page document that laid out the purposes, techniques, approaches, rationales, and permissible limits of interrogation. Less than a decade later, the strategies in this Field Manual would serve to make a brutal nightmare of Mohamedou Ould Slahi's existence. *Fear-Up Approach (Harsh): In this approach, the interrogator behaves in an overpowering manner with a loud and threatening voice. The interrogator may even feel the need to throw objects across the room to heighten the source's implanted feelings of fear. This technique is to convince the source he does indeed have something to fear, that he has no option but to cooperate. Then convince the source that you are his best or only hope in avoiding or mitigating the object of his fear, such as punishment for his crimes. The fear-up (harsh) approach is usually a dead end.*

—That's not American, Sam. We go for the win!

And still lose.

—It is brutally hot, don't you think?

— Let's watch. How awful to miss the rare success.

—I don't dare go. My bladder's the matter. I am quite your senior, need I remind you.

—It's a long trough in there, right through this tunnel, to the right. But go now, mid-inning. Men pissing their pilsner.

—Ever thus. I'm off.

When you read the whole of Beckett, even if you think you are caught going nowhere, you are going somewhere. Whether in Watt's house, in the inescapable cylinder of *The Lost Ones*, waiting interminably by a tree, on a country road, of an evening, or on the road with A and C in *Molloy*, you have a momentum if not a particular destination. Though many stories recur throughout the entire oeuvre, they are all childhood memories of one Samuel Barclay Beckett, born April 13, 1906, in the family home, Cooldrinagh, in Foxrock, County Dublin. For all the literary abstraction that seemed to be the terminus of Beckett's work—his next-to-last prose work, *Worstward Ho*, is a steady pulse of ingenious lexical negations—he never forgot the intimate tales of his own life, not tales, always, but always sensations, of being a child, of being at his mother's knee, staring up into the fierce face of May Beckett, or of walks, often hand in hand, with his father, Bill, through the Dublin hills, or having an adventure story read to him in the early evening, seeing the ships at sea or the mountain cairns or hearing "the consumptive postman" whistling on his rounds. These memories are Beckett at his most lyrical, and for all the severity and blasted landscapes that mark his plays and many of the later texts, the lyrical found purchase everywhere. No matter how abstracted the literary affects, Beckett is always writing from the source material of his own life. Indeed, his famous revelation, walking on the Dún Laoghaire East pier in 1945, he wrote, and then corrected to a shorter pier south of there, and corrected again to "my mother's room"—was that it was his self that would be his topic or at least the occasion for his explorations of the conditions and the impulse for expression. Beckett told Lawrence Harvey in 1962 that "Being is constantly putting form in danger," and that there was no form of expression Beckett knew of that didn't violate being "in the most unbearable manner." From his earliest writings, form could barely contain him— *Proust*, his first published book (at twenty-four), was "more a creative encounter between one great writer and another" than a critical monograph, wrote John Pilling. And then there are the crazy stories that made their way into *More Pricks Than Kicks*, pieces that showed a restless brilliance at war with conventional language and form. Beckett, not unlike Proust, considered being, or self itself, to be "the real originator of disorder," as the helpful Pilling puts it. Although it is not uncommon to see passages such as the well-known sucking-stone incident in *Molloy* cited as evidence of the self's gallant (if absurd) attempt to render some order in the world, the larger point of Beckett's work seems to be that Being is going to thrash form at every turn. It's not that form is oppressive to Beckett—it is as beloved as routine!—and that's what makes Beckett funny, that contradiction, that paradoxical accommodation.

I was in love so-called and about to make a big decision. I was in trouble. I summoned you somehow, in the car driving south, like Aeneas his father's ghost. I said to the small compartment of air in the car, Father would know the county, and there you were, beside me, your left arm extended over the back of the driver's seat, behind me, as was your style when riding shotgun, it let you sit up, over your gut, it helped you breathe, and you gave me your approval. You said, Wyoming. We are in Wyoming County. I took your word. Irishmen always know their counties, wherever they are, and I welcomed your approval, with some tears, it is true, which made you disappear, embarrassed you were, but I took your word, and cried, and now I have other voices in my life. Tears, I have found, silence the old voices. Perhaps it makes them sad, the old voices. And they are far beyond being sad. They have not returned merely to hear us weep, the old voices, they take silence.

In 1992, Mohamedou Ould Slahi interrupted his studies to join the insurgency against the Communist-led, Russia-backed government in Afghanistan. The US opposed this government as well. Slahi was trained in Khost and swore an oath of allegiance to al-Qaeda. *My goal was solely to fight against the aggressors, mainly the Communists, who forbid my brethren to practice their religion.* Slahi has said that after the Communists withdrew from Afghanistan, the mujahedeen began to fight among themselves—*to wage Jihad against themselves*, he put it—so he decided to return to Germany. In 2000, after more than a decade living in Germany and Canada, Slahi returned home to Mauritania, where he found himself under suspicion in connection to the Millennium Plot to bomb LAX, which was foiled by sharp-eyed US Customs agents in Port Angeles, Washington, on December 14, 1999. In 2000 and through the first eight months of 2001, Slahi was detained and interviewed several times—by Senegalese police, Mauritanian authorities, and the FBI—regarding the Millennium Plot. He was questioned again, less than three weeks after 9/11, by the FBI—regarding the Millennium Plot. At last he was declared innocent. But in late November 2001, Slahi was questioned again and taken by the CIA to Amman, Jordan, where he was interrogated for seven and a half months. Mohamedou Ould Slahi has not been home to Mauritania since, unless you call Guantanamo Prison home, where he has been since August 2002. His 122,000-word diary, handwritten in English—his fourth language—was edited by human rights activist Larry Siems and published by Little, Brown in 2015. [Slahi was finally released in October 2016. —Ed.]

—Is Barney happy with the film?
—I know he's thrilled. Getting you and Keaton together is triumph enough. But he thinks it'll do well in the festivals. As do I.
　　—It got toward something, I do think that. Buster was a great pro. I'm not sure anyone else could have done as well. He never flinched.

In 1981, journalist Larry Shainberg, out of the blue and with no introduction, sent Beckett a copy of a book he'd written, on brain surgery. Shainberg, with whom I had a drink recently, in the old style, in the lounge of a hotel, said he was surprised that the Nobel Prize winner, known to be a very private man, responded. Indeed, Beckett was quite interested in Shainberg's book. "Where do they

put the skull bone while they are working inside?"
Shainberg was a lucky guy. Beckett agreed to meet
him in London, where *Endgame* was in rehearsal
with Rick Cluchey's San Quentin players. Shainberg
was invited to the theater and got to see Beckett
in his milieu, greeting well-wishers and longtime
collaborators like Billie Whitelaw, Alan Schneider,
and Irene Worth. Shainberg was very moved
by the Beckett he saw "incarnate." He found the
experience "inspiring and disheartening, terrifying,
reassuring, and humbling in the extreme."

Enough of that. We are disturbed here, in our nest,
quite often. We are of the world, in it, and what we
can control here—the blinds, the linens, I will call
them linens, our toilette and array of unguents, reading
material, and, to some considerable extent, not to be
discounted, our moods, are all that we can do against a
brute, indifferent world. Certainly a disinterested world,
with no rooting interest in our fate, but an *un*interested
world as well. I trend in a certain direction, once I get
going. When my beloved remarked at how I so often
struggled like a blind man to find the right word for
something—carmine, say, for the color of that single
drop of blood beaded on the eye socket of a trap-
caught mouse in the foyer—I determined to find the
word for that which describes me: "pedant," she said,
"look no further, you're a pedant." To return to those
outer phenomena that disturb us—the pounding of
mysterious demolitions and constructions that go on
beyond our doors, the civil torment, the traffic, the
boom of detonations connected to road work, the weed-

whacking of a neighbor, and the other guy's fucking beagles, down the street, barking at imagined attackers. I think of Bachelard in these instances, and succor my beloved with such an anecdote, that the good Parisian first thought in his process of mind that woodpeckers, say, working on a nearby tree with a woodpecker's intensity, were but the sounds of a garden worker. And so, when his neighbor insists on banging nails hours on end in some construction, he sees him, too, as a garden worker.

In Mauritania, there is slavery still. In Mauritania, there is torture in the prisons, still. In Mauritania, ninety percent of the land is desert. In 1981, Mauritania abolished slavery. Only in 2007 did Mauritania pass a law criminalizing the owning of another person. In 2012, CNN reported that ten–twenty percent of the population, in Mauritania, remained enslaved. In Mauritania, the population is about four million. In Mauritania, the literacy rate is fifty percent. People live on a dollar and a half a day, in the Islamic Republic of Mauritania.

—A face of granite, eyes of a sad hound, that Buster.
    —That's good, Dick, very good. Now you've made me think of our old Kerry Blue, though . . . Mother put her down. Buster . . . good name for a dog.
    —Some things last forever.
—I'll quote you.

From all that I have read, if you got to know Samuel Beckett, you liked him—he was good company in his quiet way. Both shy and relaxed, funny and strict, he was always good-hearted, except when crossed by bumbling or censorious publishers and theater agents. He always had his good reasons for being unpleasant. To know Beckett, or to know his work, as Shainberg became well aware, is also to risk falling under the spell of his style. "Writers with Beckett too much in mind," Shainberg wrote, "can sound worse than the weakest student in a freshman writing class. . . . "

That's my woodworker working on the acacia tree, thinks Bachelard, *a method for obtaining calm when things disturb me.* This helps us. For some years we would access the traveling theme, "deep travel" our friend Tony calls it, and he would know—his father was a long time in jail—though for us it was deeper than that, deep as sleep, where true travel happens, not something that settles for, say, awareness. No. I could put my beloved to sleep by Peekskill. Where we would begin is on our front step, then one-two-three to the sidewalk.

Mohamedou Ould Slahi was born on New Year's Eve, 1970, the ninth of twelve children. His father was a nomadic camel trader, who died when Mohamedou was a boy but after the family had moved to the Mauritanian capital, Nouakchott. Today, nearly half the country lives in Nouakchott. By the time he was a teen, Mohamedou had memorized the Koran. He loved soccer, and particularly the German national team. He won a scholarship to study in Germany.

—I do think The Tramp would've been too lovable. Don't you?
—Too pitiable, perhaps.

"[I]n the wake of one of Beckett's convoluted, self-mocking sentences," wrote Shainberg, "one can freeze with horror at the thought of any form that suggests 'Once upon a time,' anything, in fact, which departs from the absolute present. But if you take that notion too far you lose your work in . . . the belief that you can capture both your subject and your object in the instant of composition: 'Here I am, sitting at my desk, writing Here I am, sitting at my desk.'"

We'd imagine something not forcing us out of town, no towering infernos, no rising tides, no threats of a cyclone, for that would do little to bring on sleep. Rather, a journey of exploration, from point A, which we love, our city home, to point B, which we love, mountains and trees and back roads. "The soft hills of my first home," my beloved once wrote, on her birthday it was.

The brothers in the block felt bad for me. I was dreaming almost every night that I had received mail from my family. I always passed on my dreams to my next-door neighbors, and the dream interpreters always gave me hope, but no mails came.

—And misery hates pity.

Larry mentioned this to me at the Marlton Hotel lounge, as if it was a common thing to understand, and yet I realized at that moment that I had no idea how to be free of "Beckett's convoluted, self-mocking sentences" or the economy of his comic timing (Vladimir: "I can't go on like this." Estragon: "That's what you think.").

One step leads to another, follows upon another, a wise way to go forth in life, I read it on a manhole cover— one thing followed by another is about as complex as it need be if you are lucky and not greedy, and we were not greedy, very lucky.

"I dreamt that you got a letter from your family," was a common phrase from brothers in the block.

IV.

—You'll have to excuse my dental whistle: wobbly
molar.

> I wanted to be astute enough to detect the illogic of
> the most innocent of expressions and the surprising
> logic of same (Clov: "I'll leave you." Hamm: "No!"
> Clov: "What is there to keep me here?" Hamm: "The
> dialogue.").

So set out.

> **Allegation:** That military interrogators improperly used
> duct tape to cover a detainee's mouth and head.

—Do you want to see someone over here, a dentist?
Judith could arrange it.
  —It's an abomination in there, like a vandalized
graveyard—a bevy of broken stonework.

> It is hard *not* to imitate, I told Larry. Look, I did
> the following, writing under the influence of Mr.
> Beckett: *One spring, it was spring cleaning, nothing*
> *but industry around this house, the one in which I*
> *spent my early years, by the grace of some strange*

49

relations, perhaps my parents, I was never sure, only of Gramps I was sure, that's what he told me to call him, when I could understand such orders and follow them. There it is—the hesitant, lilting, uncertain voice, nostalgic for some vanished simplicity—but the real thing, the Beckett tone, is everywhere unmatchable.

We walk to the west one hundred yards or so to where the mighty Hudson River courses by us headed south, and we take a right, or so I narrate, and walk up that river, bearing north, step after step—and then I switch gears, and we are at our garage up on Houston Street, yes, near the piers, my love, and we settle into the seats of our carriage, and adjust them, and tune to a radio station, depending, something obscure, like jazz, or corny, or brazen political talk, or guys talking about cars, unless the locals are playing. This we do without leaving the bedsheets, the pallet, or the hooked rug, depending on our fortunes. Lessens our footprint, and frees our minds, gives us cars and travel and a country home, as if we had them, and what's the difference?

Finding: Sometime in October duct tape was used to "quiet" a detainee. **Technique**: Unauthorized.

—That inning took less than five minutes.

—They all seem in a hurry. Up and down, get me home.

—I prefer to think of the precisions on display.

—Have it your way, Sam. But I hope you get to see a home run.

The Unmatchable, then, from *Texts for Nothing, 2,*
since I need it: *Above is the light, the elements, a*
kind of light, sufficient to see by, the living find their
ways, without too much trouble, avoid one another,
unite, avoid the obstacles, without too much trouble,
seek with their eyes, close their eyes, halting without
halting, among the elements, the living. Unless it has
changed, unless it has ceased. The things too must
still be there, a little more worn, a little even less,
many still standing where they stood in the days of
their indifference. Here you are under a different
glass, not long habitable either, it's time to leave it.
You are there, there it is, where you are will never
long be habitable. Go then, no, better stay, for
where would you go, now that you know?

One of the joys of such travel is looking into other
people's homes. I do remember, as a boy sitting in the
backseat of some Packard or Plymouth, folks up front,
driving around, looking into other people's homes.
Mother was particularly sharp at this. Look at those
curtains! Or, Do they have to burn *every* light? I would
peer in as homes passed by and as an exercise of mind
imagine in a flash all that I saw being intimate with
my experience, what it was like to play in the lee of
that porch or gambol about the slope of *that* hill or
be within *that* cellar from which a warm light glowed
or on *that* tar roof, near the chimney stack, warm to
my palm, looking into my own bedroom, on the third
floor, private, remote, full of sports equipment and
toy cars and seeing there a version of myself asleep.
These exercises as a youth developed in me a gift for

spitiromancing, as in reading homes, from the Greek—
spiti, house—and I noticed as the years passed and
I embarked on these passages the powerful sense, as
home after home passed, of something very familiar, as
if I had been there once in the deepest way, knew the
smells or the damp or the sound of the furnace kicking
on in that very home and where to find the cookies and
the 3-in-1 oil and where the light switch was in my
room and in every room, on the right as I walked into
the bathroom, with my knuckle.

> **Discussion**: In his testimony, the Chief testified that
> he had a situation in which a detainee was screaming
> resistance messages and potentially provoking a riot.
> At the time of the incident there were ten detainees in
> the interrogation section and the Chief was concerned
> about losing control of the situation. He directed the MPs
> to quiet the detainee down. The MP mentioned that he
> had duct tape. The Chief says he ultimately approved the
> use of the duct tape. The MP then placed a single strand
> of duct tape around the detainee's mouth—this proved
> ineffective.

—Beyond the boundary, you mean? Is that six runs?
   —Six? No, one, plus the runners on base ahead of
him, bases loaded, as we say.
   —Is it rare, beyond the boundary?
   —Is it rare in cricket?
   —It's a wondrous thing, to clear the boundary. To
be wished.
   —The record here is sixty-one in a season, four in
a game.

Where would you go, now that you know, now
that you know that where you are is no longer
habitable? Where would you go if there is nowhere
to go? Or if you know of nowhere to go? Such
questions—they might be statements, or guesses, or
even entertainments—are so common in Beckett's
work as to be implied. How old were you when
you first looked up the word *aporia*? To each his
own, I was nineteen or twenty and reading, I can't
remember, *Murphy* or *The Unnamable*. I looked the
word up in my college dictionary, we all got college
dictionaries as graduation presents in those days,
and I even brought mine to Ireland, a young chap
from a small town bringing his words across the
sea. *Aporia*: an internal irresolvable conflict. Yes, it
was *The Unnamable*, the shattering ending, a near
auto-asphyxiation, but an escape: "You must go on,
I can't go on, I'll go on."

I wound my way into other people's homes. My beloved
thrilled to this tack, as each time, I suppose, it held
the promise of a revelation. For my past she did not
know like the gospels, and with each telling some new
juicy bit might emerge, some inconsistency even, or
a glittering facet she'd call "gold." Wending, perhaps
winding, wiling my way, in any event, like an orphan
child, into one household after another, every feature
of which attests to a missing attachment, something
uncoupled, unmet, an armature waiting for its hook,
a plug dangling from an appliance. There was the big
family that took me in—did I fancy the elder daughter?
There was the bigger family that took me in—didn't

I marry the elder daughter? There was the biggest family that took me in—why did I not marry the elder daughter? There was the orphaned elder daughter I ran from. There were the parents who went off to die, those parents who took me in sight unseen. Gold?

> The detainee was yelling again. This time the MPs wrapped a single strand of duct tape around the mouth and head of the detainee. This proved ineffective. Fed up and concerned that the detainee's yelling might cause a riot in the interrogation trailer, the Chief ordered MPs to wrap the duct tape *twice* around the head and mouth and *three times* under the chin and around the top of the detainee's head. According to an FBI agent, he and another FBI agent were approached by the Chief who was laughing and told the agents that they needed to see something. When the first agent went to the interrogation room he saw that the detainee's head had been wrapped in duct tape over his beard and hair. According to the first agent, the Chief said the interrogator had done so because the detainee refused to stop "chanting" passages from the Koran. **Organizational response**: The Chief was verbally admonished by a female commander. He did not receive any formal discipline. There is no evidence that duct tape was ever used again on a detainee.

—What I love about team sport is that it has meaning only by consensus.

    —I don't follow you, Sam.

    —Smart. What is today's attendance at this match?

—They're still coming in. These seats here will be filled soon I'd guess. Maybe twenty thousand. There's a second game.

—Assuming that this one finds closure. Boxing's a different matter, I always thought. Kind of the heart of every sport.

—I suppose.

—Like chess. Your boy Fischer sacrificed his queen to win a match—hardly a consensus move. His own.

And Beckett did go on, he wasn't lying. Plays, stories, poems, novels, novellas, radio plays, film scripts, TV scripts, essays, reviews, thousands upon thousands of letters. It is true, he did not reach his aporia until after the war—he finished *L'Innommable* in 1950, the English translation came a few years later. The book, really the three novels, marked the end of Beckett as novelist, no matter various publishers' efforts in later years to frame later short prose pieces as "novels." He honored his own achievement by never writing long-form prose again. The stasis or stalling within that form meant the death of it for him, but not the death of Being. What followed was not silence of course—as much as Beckett may have wished for it he always knew he was incapable of it—but a surprising variety, an inventiveness, and a new interest: literary abstraction. Lawrence Harvey, a professor of English at Dartmouth, became a good friend of Beckett's while writing his essential study, *Samuel Beckett: Poet and Critic*. It was Harvey, in his notes on his conversations with Beckett in Paris, who wrote that Beckett thought Being was a great challenge to form. Harvey felt that Beckett was "anti-form, if form is considered to be order." Beckett favored a "disordered form, a broken form. . . . Being is chaotic, the opposite of ordered form," wrote Harvey.

At moments—and this is, ironically, my crowning success—my beloved will be asleep. I can sense the stillness, her weight evenly distributed on the bedsheets or on the pallet or the rug, deadweight warm but cooling. So she is out, and there I am, even when convinced of my triumph, feeling a need to go on. Rather, an inability to stop, since the story, no matter how poorly constructed, is alive and wriggling and will not itself be put down. And there I tell my secrets, ah yes. And then I tell my secrets. These are dark fears, I admit, that come to the surface in a quiet room with no auditor. Oh, I have confessed more truths to an empty confession box than one occupied by dear Father Norm. I suppose I was speaking with God, but He never said a thing, so I could allow myself to think He was otherwise engaged. In the morning, with light slivering in and slowly revealing our soft bedscape, my beloved still asleep, I will carry on if indeed I had ever stopped. I will go on, with prepared remarks, to usher her into the day. Something familiar and warm.

Pride and Ego-Up Approach: This approach is most effective on sources with little or no intelligence, or on those who have been looked down upon for a long time. It is very effective on low-ranking enlisted personnel and junior grade officers, as it allows the source to finally show someone that he does indeed have some intelligence. The source is constantly flattered into providing certain information to gain credit. The interrogator must take care to use a flattering, somewhat-in-awe tone of voice, and to speak highly of the source throughout this approach. This quickly produces positive feelings on the source's part, as he had probably been looking for this type of recognition all his life. Officer: *"You know, sometimes we arrest people for the wrong thing, but it turns out they are involved in something else!"* Source: *"When are you going to stop playing this game on me? Every time there is a new suspicion, and when that turns out to be incorrect, I get a new one, and so on and so forth. Is there a possibility in the world that I am involved in nothing?"* Officer: *"Of course; therefore, you have to cooperate and defend yourself. All I am asking is that you explain some shit to me."*

—Another is out. The whole side, a succession of small failures . . . leading to nothing.

—Nothing is more real than nothing, if I may quote you.

—Democritus was the tip of the spear there.

—You know, even a good hitter makes an out seven out of ten times.

—Handsome odds!

—Witness that failure, Sam. Kranepool, striking out. . . .

—*Kraaannne-pooool.*

57

Samuel Beckett produced consistently original work for sixty years, bracketed on each end by a poem: the award-winning "Whoroscope" in 1930 and 1989's near-deathbed "Comment Dire," or "What Is the Word?" (*seem to glimpse –/ need to seem to glimpse –/ afaint afar away over there what –/ folly for to need to seem to glimpse afaint afar away over there what –/ what –/ what is the word –// what is the word*). None of the work could have been written by anyone else. Even the undisciplined, precocious, anxious early stories, when Beckett did not know he would make a career as an author (he thought he might work for Sergei Eisenstein in Moscow) bear his mark. During those six decades his work changed in many ways as he ran through genres and forms, exhausting them all, but ever going on, inexhaustible himself, clearly, to the very end. Reception of his work, harsh and dismissive early on, when received at all—the publisher rejections of his early works numbered in the dozens—evolved into an industry, critical, popular, academic, political, philosophical, and even medical. Keeping up with his challenging production was one thing, and praise came from interesting quarters throughout (Adorno's essay on *Endgame*) as did ridicule (John Updike parodied Beckett's *How It Is* in the *New Yorker*). But serious scholars, aware that Beckett had become a colossal figure, did their best to co-opt him, or at least situate him within various movements that suited one purpose or another. Beckett was ill-served by these attempts, however well-intentioned, as surely many of them were.

I will give her a favorite, from both our childhoods, from Stevenson's *Garden of Verses*. *My bed is like a little boat,* I say quietly, *nurse helps me in when I embark. She girds me in my sailor's coat and starts me in the dark. At night, I go on board and say, Good-night to all my friends on shore. I shut my eyes and sail away and see and hear no more. And sometimes things to bed I take, as prudent sailors have to do. Perhaps a slice of wedding-cake, perhaps a toy or two. All night across the dark we steer, but when the day returns at last, safe in my room, beside the pier, I find my vessel fast.* My beloved will awake, either hungry or inclined to play.

> **Allegation**: That military interrogators improperly chained detainees and placed them in a fetal position on the floor. **Finding**: On at least two occasions, detainees were "short shackled" to the eyebolt on the floor in the interrogation room. **Technique**: Unauthorized. **Discussion**: Short-shackling is the process by which the detainee's hand restraints are connected directly to an eyebolt in the floor requiring the detainee to either crouch very low or lay in a fetal position on the floor. One agent stated that she witnessed a detainee short-shackled and lying in his own excrement. There was no documentation, testimony, or other evidence corroborating another agent's recollection that one of the detainees had pulled out his hair while short-shackled. **Organizational response**: None. **Recommendation**: The allegation should be closed. No

evidence to adequately assign responsibility for these actions was found.

—I think there is a lot to explore in containment.

—How so, Sam?

—I can't eat these, I regret to say. My teeth. I'll suck the salt off them.

—You mean like Robbe-Grillet, writing only about objects?

—Christ, no.

Beckett was sixteen years old when the Irish Free State was formed, in 1922, and he died just as the Soviet Union collapsed in 1989. In the duration of his adult life there were two world wars, a genocide in Europe, a cultural revolution, in France and elsewhere, and the attainment of a country's presidency by a playwright and friend, Václav Havel (he wrote a play for Havel, *Catastrophe*). Now that he has been dead a quarter century, Beckett is being exhumed from the many movements that claimed him for their own. Early on, he was able to shake off these claimants himself, denouncing the romantic poetry of Ireland in an early review and, much later, responding to a reporter's question, Do you consider yourself an English writer? with "Au contraire." But in postwar France, his work was critically situated in such a way that proved difficult to controvert, it took such a hold. It has taken decades to do so.

When she stirs, in whatever mood or inclination, it is another miracle. A gift. For no one carries on alone, or this one does not at least. That is the secret I do not divulge—that the lone wanderer can never be alone. Perhaps she sees this, and it is widely known. But I have my myths to maintain!

There are two types of rapport postures determined during planning and preparation: stern and sympathetic. In the stern posture, the interrogator keeps the detainee at attention. The aim is to make the detainee keenly aware of his helpless and inferior status. In the sympathetic posture, the interrogator addresses the detainee in a friendly fashion, striving to put him at ease. Frightened persons, regardless of rank, will invariably talk in order to relieve tension. When making promises in an effort to establish rapport, great care must be taken to prevent implying that rights guaranteed the detainee under international law will be withheld if the detainee refused to cooperate.

—Why can't that organist play some Schubert?
 —Funny. I'll have Judith ring the press box.
 —"Fugue in E Minor," please.

The problem was France, a country that emerged from WWII in shame. Paris had fallen to the Nazis in eight days. Beckett, after fleeing the Gestapo and hiding out in the French countryside for three years, returned to a liberated Paris and wrote four form-shattering masterpieces—*Waiting for Godot* and the Trilogy—by 1950.

Still, the fears are mixed with desires. I read that somewhere. What you fear you want.

Things went more quickly than I thought. The Escort team showed up at my cell. "You got to move."

—Four innings in, Sam, no score.

Vichy.

Homelessness.

"Where?"

V.

—Could I nick one of those Lucky Strikes off you?
Smoked these in Saint-Lô, you know, though the
pack was green, as I recall, not red.

"[A] being without being, who can neither live
nor die, stop nor start, the empty space in which
the idleness of an empty speech speaks," wrote
Maurice Blanchot of the figure in *The Unnamable in
Nouvelle review française*, October 1953.

I know the end to this story; we all do.

During the course of interrogations, certain detainees
exhibited refined resistance to interrogation.

—Yep, here you go.
　　—Have you a spark? [*Inhaling deeply*] Finer than
a Woodbine, [*exhaling*] but no Gitane.

"What Molloy reveals is not simply reality but reality
in its pure state: the most meager and inevitable
of realities, that fundamental reality continually
soliciting us, but from which a certain terror always
pulls us back. . . . There is in this reality the essence

or residue of being," wrote Georges Bataille in *Critique*, 1951.

Although the premise and hope of a beginning such as this is that we do not know the end, we do: it ends in mystery. I could say silence but what is that?

> These detainees who exhibited refined resistance techniques were suspected of possessing significant current intelligence regarding planned future terrorist attacks. For these reasons, Special Interrogation Plans were carried out and they are referred to as "First Special Interrogation Plan" and "Second Special Interrogation Plan."

—If they get this inning in the game is official.
　—*C'est complet?*
　—I mean, were bad weather to halt it—not that we expect that today—it would be an official game, and would count.
　—But we are still at love.
　—True. But you get my point.

> Wrote Marjorie Perloff in the *Iowa Review*, 2005: "[F]or the first wave of Beckett critics in postwar France—critics for whom war memories were not only painful but embarrassing, given the collaboration of the Vichy government—it was preferable to read Beckett as addressing man's alienation and the human condition rather than anything as specific as everyday life in the years of the Resistance." Why is this important? Why do I care? We fast-forward to today: the editor-in-chief of the *Journal of Beckett Studies*, Dirk Van Hulle,

agrees that the critical construction of the "universal Beckett" in the postwar years, mostly in France, a kind of ahistorical Beckett, is no longer relevant.
It gave way, in the 1980s and '90s, to "capital-T Theory," Adorno, Deleuze, Kristeva, Derrida, etc. (And is still around, in the figure of Alain Badiou, who has come to see Beckett as an anti-Platonist exploring the limits of logical systems such as mathematics.)

I have never known silence. There is no such thing, for the living, but that's where I am headed. A silence beyond sound. A metaphorical silence, where there is no space, no time, no matter. The end.

The subject was forced to wear a woman's bra and had a thong placed on his head during the course of investigation: **Authorized**. The subject was told that his mother and sister were whores: **Authorized**. The subject was told that he was a homosexual, had homosexual tendencies, and that other detainees had found out about these tendencies: **Authorized**. An interrogator tied a leash to the subject, led him around the room, and forced him to perform a series of dog tricks: **Authorized**. An interrogator forced the subject to dance with a male interrogator: **Authorized**. The subject was forced to stand naked for five minutes with females present: **Authorized**.

—I don't wish to come back . . . to Amerikay. I hope Barney understands.

—Never, Sam? Don't say never.

—I don't know, but there might be, god help us, some publicity attached at some point. Thereto. To *Film*?

—I could take you to a better ballgame! But I get it . . .

—I don't appreciate the systems here, everything's new, viscid, as if not yet formed or set. Paris is old. It's . . . comfortably ossified.

What dominates Beckett studies today is the parallel play of those critics who dilate upon what Van Hulle, taking a term from *Murphy*, calls "the demented particulars"—Beckett's Ireland, his family, his war experience, his politics, his library—and those critics who see Beckett as an abstract artist who happens to be working in words. Van Hulle: "On the one hand, this implies an enhanced attention to the historical circumstances. . . . [And] on the other hand, this renewed attention to particulars . . . dovetails with the recent 'cognitive turn' in several disciplines within the humanities, notably in narrative theory." But that's really not what Van Hulle means, is it? As it turns out (we read on), what he means is something more complex, less simple and binary, though we have to hang in there to find out—and it seems true, once said: "What makes Beckett studies so vibrant today is the interaction among different approaches, ranging from theory to contextual, historical to archival research. . . . [W]e have moved beyond . . . black-and-white." But that's no good for me. I am asking *why Beckett?* My beloved is gently inquiring *why Beckett.* Multifarious reasons won't fly for long, life is too short. There must be a reason *why Beckett.*

Silence as sleep. How do I know when to stop telling my story, one might ask. How is it I know when my beloved has been delivered into—may I?—the arms of Morpheus? Her sleep—it is not silence—is heralded by a sound, a nearly inaudible "pop" or "puh" from her lips, as they separate ever so slightly when sleep has possessed the body, of which the face is the signal part in this instance, and it has relaxed, fallen into repose, as it were. Aspirate. Say it: *aspirate*. Little else moves when a certain level of consciousness takes its leave but her lips producing this "pop" or "puh." That which has coursed within her body, surely her chest cavity, the whole phonatory column, has escaped into the room we are in. One might think a change in the rhythm of breathing would be another bit of evidence, and I made this impoverished assumption myself, and still do, on occasion, but it is never so much determinative as born of my hope.

On several occasions, the subject was subjected to strip searches, which the subject himself later characterized as "cavity searches": **Authorized**. On seventeen occasions, interrogators poured water over the subject's head: **Authorized**. **Discussion**: The subject was a high-value detainee that ultimately provided extremely valuable intelligence. His ability to resist months of standard interrogation in the summer of 2002 was the genesis for the request to have the authority to employ additional counter-resistance techniques, approved by the Secretary of Defense. Interrogators believed they were acting within existing guidance and indeed their techniques were legally permissible, though an investigation concluded that the "creative, aggressive, and persistent" interrogation of the subject constituted "degrading and abusive treatment." The report cited as "particularly troubling" the combined impact of six months' segregation, forty-eight of fifty-four consecutive days of eighteen-to-twenty-hour interrogation, and the other "creative" techniques, such as the thong, the bra, the prolonged nakedness in front of female interrogators, not to mention the presence of WMDs, which in this context means "working military dogs."

—I can live with the dead. I should be in Venice. You know Suzanne told me that. Pound's over there flaking like a relic.

—People die in New York, Sam. They *are* dying, and overseas.

—But that's well struck! There's life yet, you are right. [*Chanting*] Let's go Mets!

—How is Suzanne?

—Grand, and busy, with Anne and Avigdor since I left.

—Jeanette would love to see her again.

You can do things straight and you can do things crooked. Someone said that. Direct or oblique. And those are the directed actions, the willed assaults. There is also chance. What a complex relationship we have with chance! The most important text on Beckett I have ever read I came upon by chance—at a publisher's luncheon for a mystery writer who had published a nonfiction book with a left-wing press on the literature of dissent—I was there by professional obligation, as a member of the trade press. There I saw a woman I hadn't seen in years—she was now the publicist for this left-wing press, and last I'd seen her she was organizing a book distribution company for none other than John Calder, Beckett's British publisher of longstanding. She had several of her company's titles at the luncheon, and, recalling her Calder days perhaps, handed me a slim volume by one Pascale Casanova titled *Samuel Beckett: Anatomy of a Literary Revolution*. I read that short book that evening, and then began again. I then ordered nine copies and sent them to selected friends.

I may be more than ready to quit, say, the lurid Le Fanu or one of my own travelogues, and sense I hear or even feel a slight settling of her rib cage, and then slowly halt my reading, if I am reading, or my story, if I am weaving a tale, only to hear, "and then what?" So now I wait for the "pop" or "puh" to find my end. *Aspirate.* . . . Mercifully, *good* stories bear repetition without sacrifice of potency. But these must be chosen wisely, for not all are good in the sense I intend, nor do their effects not wear off, either on the very evening of their delivery, or, if overdone, by their very commencement: "Not that one!" What have I learned that works best? The aforesaid cycle of the seasons, perhaps each a little differently—I can't say a little seasoned, though wish to—a little altered in presentation, say, is a winner. As are various ditties about my childhood, so innocent, so far distant,

so irrelevant because so over. The tale of my first
trout, yes; the little doggie my parents adopted and
surrendered, due to its errant bowels and proclivity
to nip, yes; the old folks in town, Julius, Black Albert,
Paul Favaro, who spoke only French, *oui*. In fact,
I had a dream last night, about Paul, poor fellow,
rest in peace, in which I bought this man, our small
town's most destitute and perhaps beloved citizen,
leathery, weathered face, his person always garbed in
heavy cotton green work clothes, surviving on some
disability check, favoring a six-pack of Genessee each
day and a pack of Camels, but, in this dream, moved
into the future, into his unrealized future by my
present adulthood, he appeared last night in a large
urban place where I looked out for him and clearly
recall I bought him, from a nearby delicatessen, a ham
sandwich, I decided on lettuce for him, and mustard,
and a bottle of Budweiser, and a bag of Wise potato
chips, a pack of smokes, and brought them to him.
I took care of Paul Favaro, last night. Another story,
note it.

> "I'm gonna show you the evidence bit by bit," he said.
> "There is a big guy who told us that you are involved."
> Mohamedou: "I guess you shouldn't ask me questions
> then, since you have a witness. Just take me to court
> and roast me. What have I done, according to your
> witness?" "He said you are part of the conspiracy."
> Mohamedou wrote: "The 'big guy' who testified against
> me turned out to be someone who was said to have said
> that I helped him get to Chechnya with two other guys
> who were among the hijackers. But then I knew about

*the horrible torture that this big guy had suffered after
his arrest. Eyewitnesses who were captured with him
thought he was dead. They heard his moans and cries
day and night."*

—Speaking of the dead—old Brendan.

—Bless, barely forty, but he drank a century's
worth and was awake for most of it.

—Can I tell you how I tried—in vain I gather—to
keep him from your door, back in the '50s? He'd read
my piece on your work in *Merlin*.

—Jerome told me you did your best, but he's a
grander force then we.

—He nearly drank and ate me out of all I had.
But he made up for it in song.

—That he did, I'm sure. I wrote a tribute to
Brendan, in *Theaterheute*.

Pascale Casanova (a name worthy of Nabokov)—
gender-bending, high-brow, a touch lascivious that
name, like perhaps a nomme d'amour or de guerre,
is in fact the name of a French literary scholar,
now a visiting professor in Romance Languages at
Duke University. She is best known for her rather
speculative book, *The World Republic of Letters*, in
which the history of literature is treated as a kind
of survival-of-the-fittest contest, with dominant
narratives suffering assaults from the periphery. In
her book on Beckett, she razes the critical ground
around her, leveling Maurice Blanchot and Georges
Bataille and others along the way, especially those
who have subdued the challenging work of Beckett

to their own purposes, most crucially in the postwar period. What got lost—and Casanova, to my mind, is the one who discovered this or at least said it most plainly and first—is "the meaning of [Beckett's] literary project," which she claims (and adduces) unfolded over his six decades of work. "The literary abstraction he invented," she writes, "at the cost of a lifetime's enormous effort, [was] in order to put literature on a par with all the major artistic revolutions of the twentieth century—especially pictorial abstraction. . . . " Casanova claims that Beckett's search for a form to accommodate Being as he understood it was systematic—all impasses he encountered were escaped through abstraction. And in his penultimate prose work, *Worstward Ho*, he reached his most radical abstraction, a kind of linguistic engineering, almost a new language, a morphemic cocktail centered on negation. "One of the greatest literary revolutions of the twentieth century," wrote Casanova. No one had said this with any specificity before.

It has not been lost on me that *The Arabian Nights*, Scheherazade's sinuous succession of tales, were meant to stave off Scheherazade's own execution. It is not that her thousand-and-one tales were meant to keep the emperor awake, exactly—the dead opposite to my commission—but, with each story, to keep the treacherous man so involved in the narrative as to make him beg in his heart for continuance, night after night. And each night, one tale would conclude, and cleverly, Scheherazade would begin another, a cliff-hanger, of sorts, to ensure another day of life. I trotted out this tale of the Tales to my beloved, and rightly confused was she, as with tables turned and obversions of intent, she made to be awake with agitation, so these issues I came to ponder in private. But mark me it did and deeply, this connection. It troubled me, it is fair to say. And the more so, as I skimmed in my leisure at a rural English university the sixteen-volume Nouvelle Revue Française edition of *À la recherche du temps perdu* owned by one Samuel Beckett, a handwritten notation on the very last page of the very last volume that read thus: "Arabian nights of the mind" and "Thought: *jellyfish* of the spirit." I determined in an instant that this described my commission for my nocturnal narratives—to be spineless, amorphous, a translucent substance in a transparent medium, the transit of dreams, adrift. This would put anyone to sleep.

> Speaking in dazed, frightened, and staccato voices, survivors of the coordinated Paris attacks have begun recalling the sickening horror of a truly nightmarish Friday the 13th. The terrorists struck almost simultaneously in six sites in Paris—Stade de France, La Petit Cambodge restaurant and Carillon bar, Rue de la Fontaine au Roi, Bataclan concert hall, Boulevard Voltaire, and La Belle Équipe bar. The assaults began around 9:15 p.m. local time on Friday, with three suicide bombings near the Stade de France, where French President François Hollande and a crowd of 80,000 were watching a France-Germany friendly soccer game. Almost simultaneously, gunmen with automatic rifles jumped from cars near popular bars

and restaurants in the capital, shooting at Parisian diners. Those caught up in the attacks described scenes of "carnage" that some likened to a "civil war." Witnesses at the Bataclan concert hall—where at least eighty people were killed—described the terror that unfolded before their eyes at the French capital's famous music venue. One young man who managed to flee said: "I was lying in a grave, the girl next to me was dead. They were shooting repeatedly," the *Daily Express* reported. Another witness, with blood all over his jeans, said at the scene: "I had a piece of flesh on me, there was blood everywhere, bodies everywhere."

—Behan spent a night in quod years later. They had to turn around a flight to Dublin, with himself on it. He would not be consoled. Barged around the cabin right into the gendarmes.

    —Did you get a call?

    —No, poor Boris was so honored.

So leastward on. So long as dim still. Dim undimmed. Or dimmed to dimmer still. To dimmost dim. Leastmost in dimmost dim.

Blanchot's "monster without fins." Should I read to my beloved from *Thomas l'Obscur*? This book was the first to make my hair stand on end—it gave me a shiver, literally. Shall I tell that story, about a book that changed my life? No, no, no. I am still working within the corridors of her life, not mine.

Theresa Cede, a thirty-nine-year-old who works in the telecommunications sector, was also at Bataclan with a friend when the terrorists burst in, shooting people standing near her on a balcony, according to a Bloomberg report. "I hid underneath the body of a man who was shot in the head. I was covered in blood," Cede said. Another woman lying next to her was severely wounded. She said she miraculously escaped unharmed after police stormed the building. "I don't know how many guardian angels I had looking out for me," she said. All hell broke loose when four men, armed with Kalashnikov assault rifles, entered the concert hall at around 9:30 p.m., forty minutes into the band's set, after killing the bouncers, witnesses said.

—Yes, in memory of the Borstal lad.
    —Drink up.
    —It's finished.

Utmost dim. Leastmost in utmost dim.
Unworsenable worst.

I have forgotten that story, *to be perfectly honest,* as they say throughout Donegal. Or it is not important. Or it is both forgotten and unimportant.

Some of the hooded gunmen, with their faces covered by scarves, shouted in French: "All of this is your President's fault," while others spoke of France's military intervention in Syria, according to witnesses. Benoit, one of the massacre survivors, who managed to escape with a friend, said: "I thought a loudspeaker had exploded, then the lights came up. The gunmen I saw had their faces covered by hoods and scarves."

—It lingers.

This Casanovian analysis has stuck with me for a half-dozen years.

But how would I know what I know?

People hit the ground as panic and terror suddenly replaced the fun they were having.

VI.

—You know, the New York pitcher has a no-hitter
going.

Then I read this, further on in *Worstward Ho*:
"Nothing and yet a woman."

Time and duration I wish to re-experience, where all
the stories are.

The four gunmen took hostages.

—I thought you said it was rare? Is this history, will
this be written in the books . . . or at least in your
Daily News?
—No!

It is not totally abstract, Beckett's language, and not
by fault. Even this most mature and near-final work,
a text that certainly is his most abstract, is, at the
end, visited by a figure, a woman, and then, a child,
and then, a man. They enter this arid wordscape,
embodied, carnate, irreducible.

But I can do so only through space. I walk through my spaces, ambulatory now, where time is condensed, but there is only so much space that is mine and as the stories empty the space the space disappears—white light, endless expanse beyond space that is nothingness. Language deteriorates.

> But three of the four gunmen detonated the bombs in their suicide belts, blowing up themselves and their hostages as the French special forces units attacked. The survivors among the hostages described a horrific "bloodbath" as the shootings began. One witness said: "It lasted ten or fifteen minutes. They reloaded their weapons, they were well equipped. They reloaded three or four times."

—Infield hit. Should have been ruled an error.
　　—So much for the judges.
　　—Umpires don't make those calls, Sam. A guy upstairs, in the press box.
　　—Always the guy upstairs.
　　—He called it a hit, for Lillis.

This is Being, indomitable, live and wriggling in a void. Against the abstraction I often see those dark, stooped figures—the figurative, literally, moving through, a kind of taunt to abstraction. I don't know that Beckett wanted them there intellectually— he managed to get rid of the Auditor, the dark, djellaba-clad figure written into the original *Not I*, on technical grounds (insurmountable lighting problems on the dark stage). No: I think that Beckett definitely *did not* want them there, these figures. After all, he admired, in painting, absolute absences, as in Cézanne's *Mont Sainte-Victoire* paintings, and the absolute voids in Bram van Velde's work. Or so he contended when a young man, and so he strived for as an older writer, these absences, but which, the more he managed the absences and the silences, the more he failed to stop the figures walking through, bringing presence, breaking silence. Godot never comes, true, but the Boy does, twice. One feels he will come every day, with promises of tomorrow.

What has happened, at life's halfway point? Beckett said of his *Godot*: "I wanted walls I could touch." I am in this room now, not only empty but emptied. I am alone or this is an issue of mental health. I am so sorry. Those are the walls.

Another survivor said: "Everyone was cowering and running from the shots. It was chaos—there were so many people. Then twenty to thirty shots were fired, randomly. I was walking on bodies, there was blood everywhere." Thomas, twenty-seven, described "rivers of blood" as he rushed toward the exit. "The aim was to attack and kill. Every time someone moved, we heard shots." Dozens of survivors hid in the balcony and then climbed onto the roof, escaping into a nearby apartment where they found refuge while waiting for hours for authorities to secure the area.

—I don't want sound in the film, Dick. I think I am dead certain on that. What do you think?

—Buster's a silent film star. That's justification enough for me—for the silence.

— Sidney thinks some sound will reinforce the distinction, between Eye and Object. The more I think on it the more I hear only silence. Other than the "shhh," of course, at the start. I think the images have a sheer beauty, a strangeness.

He wrote to his early art pal Thomas MacGreevy about the Cézannes he saw in London in the 1930s. "Cezanne seems to have been the first to see landscape & state it as material of a strictly peculiar order, incommensurable with all human expression whatsoever." Beckett was taken with the "unalterable alienness" between landscape and the gaze in Cézanne, which, tellingly, he configured as "the 2 solitudes." He found the space between them an "impassable immensity," and lamented to MacGreevy how there was "nothing of the kind" in Constable or Turner, in whose works "the landscape shelters or threatens or serves or destroys . . . nature is really infected with 'spirit.'" Few have looked as deeply into Beckett and painting as Mark Nixon, who is a professor at the University of Reading, which houses a massive Beckett archive. A major focus of his scholarship is the six months Beckett spent in Germany in the dark winter of 1936–37. Beckett was there to look at art and perhaps lick his wounds from a disastrous romantic summer, where he fell for an American woman named Betty Stockton, who spurned him, and then found solace with a married childhood friend who was back visiting Dublin, creating a small scandal.

Absence—such fun to play with . . . in the abstract!
But when the beloved has vanished, what does one do?
Does anyone know? Tell me the story. Tell me what it is.
I don't know that I have any stories left. Won't living be
enough? It is not enough. It is nothing.

Auralie hid in a room in the concert hall for more than
two hours. She said: "We could hear everything going on.
It was as though people were being tortured, butchered."
John, who was among those who climbed the roof to
escape, mentioned one steward who rushed to open a
door amid the gunfire, allowing people to escape onto
the roof. John said: "There were several children on the
upper floor, I had a kid and woman next to me. I was
one of the first to get out, then we pulled people up one
by one onto the metal roof—around sixty of us." Daniel
Psenny, a journalist at *Le Monde* who lives behind the
concert hall, allowed the survivors to take shelter in his
apartment as the massacre went on nearby. "I heard a
noise," he said, "like firecrackers, and I told myself it was
just in the film I was watching. But the noise was loud,
so I went to the window. I saw men lying on the ground,
blood. I realized it was something serious. Everyone
was running onto the street. I had images of 9/11 in
my head."

—It works, Sam, it really does. A film about film
titled *Film*. I think it will knock people's socks off.
    —What comes off next?
    —Hard to say. But if nobody here can score a run
we'll be here forever.
    —Life everlasting, in a ball grounds.

—Could be worse, I suppose.

—At least the plumbing works.

—I brought a pint of whiskey . . . in case of inclement weather.

—May it resume its kind offices, should the need arise.

—Amen.

Nixon has edited the *German Diaries*, six notebooks found in a trunk upon Beckett's death by his nephew. The diaries are handwritten, mostly accounts of the books Beckett read and the art he saw and his own agonies over writing. He also coolly observes the slowly constricting grip of the Nazis. It is chilling to read the young Irishman recording what it is like to listen to Hitler's harangues on the radio in 1936. Why is Beckett there, a rather lost young man though no doubt a brilliant one, already having passed through academia with great honors as well as an apprenticeship with James Joyce, to whom he was clearly helpful? Why has he wandered into Nazi Germany, torrid as it was with demagoguery, hatred, and censorship? Beckett is there alone, his former ties to a Jewish Dublin family, the Sinclairs, who had a home in Kassel, now done with—Beckett had been in love with the Sinclairs' daughter, Peggy, but she died at twenty-three of tuberculosis. Beckett befriends a bookseller, Axel Kaun, and a few others. And is, in the main, miserable. But he reads dozens of books, mostly popular fiction, and sees hundreds of paintings, most of them not nearly so popular, in fact considered by the state officially "degenerate," and writes about it all in the *German Diaries*. He also wrote letters—to MacGreevy mostly, but also to the woman I thought, for a time, had a child with Beckett. But if that was the case, either she did not tell him that the baby was his, did not know the baby was his, told him the baby was not his, or there is suppressed correspondence.

Her words began to diminish. In number. Their numbers lessened, elaborate phrases—"Mightn't you find it in your heart, in the fullness of time, to make an appointment for us with the adjustor, before rack, then ruin?"—gave way to series of locutions less involved, less wordy, but did I notice, did I mark it, did I make an appointment for us with the adjustor, or the physician, or the social office, or summon all our friends? I did not. I was telling stories, you were asking for them, I did not listen to you. All I listened for was your "puh." And now I hear it no more. In your absence . . . —my syntax my suffers. Miss I mean. Relief to. Said it. Have said it.

A Belgian parking ticket found inside a rented Volkswagen turned an investigation of seven dead suicide bombers into an international manhunt for a cell of up to twenty terrorists involved in the Paris attacks. In the hours after the wave of coordinated attacks that left 129 people dead on Friday night, French police reassured Parisians that all of the ISIL terrorists had either blown themselves up or been killed. But the investigation was turned on its head when officers examined the Belgian-registered black VW Polo left parked near the Bataclan concert hall,

where eighty-nine people had been murdered. A parking
ticket inside the car was from the Molenbeek suburb of
Brussels, notorious as a crucible of Islamic fanaticism.
It led to the discovery that the car had been rented
by the brother of one of the dead terrorists, and the
realization that more jihadists may have been involved.
By Sunday night seven men were in custody, another
was being urgently hunted and intelligence agencies
feared up to five more men could be involved. As well
as the VW Polo, police found a black Belgian-registered
SEAT Leon abandoned in the suburb of Montreuil, three
miles from the locations of the attacks. Inside the SEAT
were three Kalashnikov assault rifles, five magazines of
bullets and eleven empty magazines. A third Belgian car,
a gray VW, was stopped by French police at Cambrai,
near the Belgian border, on Saturday morning, but police
found nothing suspicious, took the occupants' names and
allowed them to carry on. It was only later in the day that
the VW Polo was linked to Belgian Salah Abdeslam, whose
older brother Ibrahim was among the seven terrorists
who died in the attacks.

—Ah! Did you see that? Hit by the pitch.
　　—If he's blocking the wicket he'd be out, at
Portora sure.
　　　—He gets a base and a run scores, in this game!
　　　—We should drink to that, Mr. Seaver.
　　　—Hear! To Ron Hunt, our all-star.
　　　—*Sláinte.*

The letters from Germany to Beckett's Dublin friend,
now living in America, pregnant with child, betray

no sense that the child is theirs. What the letters do contain, those that are published at least, is that Beckett is miserable and unable to write. And yet he writes to her with his signature concision, and he is indeed in Nazi Germany ("All the lavatory men say Heil Hitler. The best pictures are in the cellar."). A Beckett letter of November 14, 1936, begins with this paragraph: "Congratulations." The editors of the voluminous Beckett letters—perhaps the last great epistolary correspondence we will know—gloss this "Congratulations" with a footnote: "SB's reference is not known." After his congratulatory opening line (or word), Beckett added: "Praised be the day before evening. Or not at all."

It is not good to talk to one's self, however captive that audience. Love is an auditor, but not much of an editor. I don't want to hear myself. It becomes too familiar. And suspect. I move in and out of coherence, like a radio signal going in and out, mixing formats and accents and playlists. It becomes . . . senseless.

Armed police operations continued on Sunday. Two of the seven suicide bombers from Friday's attacks were Frenchmen living in Brussels, and one of the seven men being held was also French and living in the Belgian capital. Salah Abdeslam, twenty-six, became Europe's most wanted man when French police issued an international arrest warrant for him, warning the public that he is dangerous and therefore "do not intervene yourself." He and his two brothers appear to be at the heart of the terrorist cell behind the attacks.

—There'll be a while to see the edits in process, right? You don't have to decide now?

—Suzanne is arranging for a Moviola and Alan will send us a cut to look at, next month. And Barney's to be over and we can watch it together. I despair.

—Two hot dogs, right here! *Chien chaud*, Sam.

If Beckett was engaged in a sublimated exchange with his pregnant friend, then how to explain his letter's dive into talk of toilet paper, equating its sheets with book pages, and of his creative production, as he saw it, six-inch square laxatives, sheet by sheet, in the "Beckett Bowel Books . . . 1000 wipes of clean fun." Is he dramatically debasing himself in a private correspondence with a married woman he might have stained? Beckett is ostensibly talking about a publisher, George Reavey, and about being published generally as some sort of vile excretion, and he is in a rant. But further in his letter he turns more somber and talks about how "flattered" he is. "It is only from the highest unities that a third can be negligently carved away and the remainder live. The amoeba's neck is not easily broken." He concludes with, "I can't read, write, drink, think, feel, or move."

There once was a psychiatric patient who said only one word: "tan." Not bad, for one word: a color, a sign of health, of leisure perhaps, of gainful employ perhaps, out of doors—plenty of Vitamin what's it? *Something one does to animal skin.* There once was a patient who was convinced she had died.

With seven suicide bombers dead, seven others under arrest and one man on the run, fifteen men have so far been linked to the Paris attacks. But Belgian intelligence officials have suggested that up to twenty people may have been part of the terrorist cell that planned the attacks, meaning a total of six people could be on the run. According to the Belgian business newspaper *L'Echo*, the Belgian security services estimate that twenty people participated "near or far" in the Paris attacks. A Syrian passport found beside one of the Paris suicide bombers has raised the possibility one of the attackers may have masqueraded as an asylum seeker to infiltrate Europe. The passport found after the attack at France's national stadium was used to enter Greece less than two months ago along a route used by hundreds of thousands of refugees and migrants this year. The French authorities said the passport was fake.

—Through six of our innings, not that bad, eh. Hour and a half. You fine?

Hegel, I guess. Leibniz I know not. Beckett, when in Germany, never mentions Brecht, according to Mark Nixon. Isn't that strange?

I read to myself of medical mysteries. Cotard Delusion, Capgras Syndrome. All neurological disorders.

Bearing the name of Ahmad Almohammad, twenty-five, the passport was used by an asylum seeker who registered on the island of Leros on October 3. He reached Leros after his makeshift boat from Turkey carrying seventy migrants foundered off the coast and he was picked up by Greek coast guards. He then reportedly applied for asylum in Serbia on October 7 before traveling on to Croatia, Hungary, Austria, and then, it is believed, France.

—I am grand, Dick, excellent kill of an afternoon— still gloriously in its throes.

"Dear _____ , I am writing to you in a pub."

Delusions of non-existence.

A US intelligence official told CBS News it did not contain the correct numbers for a legitimate Syrian passport and the picture did not match the name.

VII.

—Up and down, up and down, three up, three down.

   To _____: "The trip is being a failure."

Missing body parts.

   A French suicide bomber who blew himself up during
   the attack on the Bataclan concert hall is believed to have
   trained at an ISIL terrorist camp in Syria.

—I'm not sure if this is going by quickly or slowly.
Lots of zeroes out there on the tote board. That's
elegant.

   "Germany is horrible," he writes to _____ . "I
   can't imagine anything worse than the mental
   marasmus, in which I totter & sweat for months. It
   has turned out indeed to be a journey *from*, and not
   to, as I knew it was, before I began it."

I have already died. I am no more. No one notices.

   Ismaël Omar Mostefaï made contact with the extremists
   in Syria after traveling through Turkey in late 2013. The
   twenty-nine-year-old was identified by DNA taken from

one of his fingers found at the scene of the deadliest of the Paris attacks. Mostefaï is thought to have returned early in 2014.

—In a normal game there's more scoring. But the pitchers Lary and Larsen are both sharp today. They've hardly walked a man. You know, the four balls. . . .

—Aye, the discordant four among this game of threes and multiples of three—three strikes, and three bases, right? But four balls make a *walk* and four bases make a *run*, am I right?

> If a journey *from* is a journey *to* you have Beckett. Can I assert that? I do say I may have learned, at the very least, after these months of reading him, that that is true. How liberating to think that this is progress! Life is not a line but a kind of wandering circle—Oh how I love, in a late work, *Ill Seen Ill Said*, the description of an old woman's cabin as "a roughly circular whole . . . as though outlined by a trembling hand."

I'm not going to be the one to tell them. Once I say so, it is suicide. The myth of living is as strong as the measure of it, and co-extensive. I am dead inside but the only one to know it. Hence the liberty of delusions.

> Mostefaï's DNA was already in France's national DNA databank because he had been arrested and convicted of a string of petty crimes while growing up in the Paris suburb of Courcouronnes, although he was never jailed. He was flagged as a potential security threat in

2010 after being radicalized in Chartres, a cathedral town southwest of Paris, reportedly by a Belgian imam. Mostefaï moved to Chartres to join one of his brothers who ran a shisha bar there, a municipal official said. Mostefaï lived in a modest terraced house with his wife and daughter, his parents, two of his brothers and his two sisters, but left for Algeria in 2012. His trace was picked up when he entered Turkey the next year. His brother Houari Mostefaï, thirty-four, was arrested and questioned after turning himself in to police on Saturday when he learned that his brother was one of the attackers.

—You might work out some musical counterpoint to this game. Some charts.

—Let it remain a sport is best. Why are we standing?

—Seventh inning stretch. Some American president got up and stretched during the seventh inning and now we all do it—and sing this song. Speaking of music.

—They cut to this tune I think in *A Night at the Opera*, from Verdi to this.

—It's playing at the Thalia uptown, near Buster's hotel.

—Nothing like standing to renew one's regard for sitting.

Beckett's journey went on, and this turns up perhaps my central question, which quite possibly covers the critical waterfront that Van Hulle mentioned: what was Beckett traveling from (those "demented particulars") and what was he traveling to (a revolutionary literary abstraction)? That is both tender and simple in concept. We all have a story; we all want a story, a narrative, a *something something*. Don't we want Beckett to be based in something, to mean something, whether it be his "particulars" or an aesthetic goal—and isn't Beckett's very evasiveness on those scores part of what fascinates? On the one hand, as he wrote, "Life alone is enough. I wanted a story. That was my mistake." On the other, the need to express, and the comfort in the pursuit of rational inquiry, or at least, of its ritual: "The same old questions, the same old answers. There's nothing like them."

One thing I pretend to know is that my beloved has come back. There she is, identical in every trace. But an impostor. Captive to Capgras? I know it. Does she? I cannot say. Still, her visible presence is a comfort. And there is one miraculous gift in this otherwise fraudulent resurrection: all my stories are new to her. Fresh snow.

> BRUSSELS — Warning of a "serious and imminent" threat of a Paris-style terrorist attack, the authorities in Belgium on Saturday shut down the Brussels subway system, canceled soccer games and advised citizens to avoid public places amid a security lockdown across the Belgian capital. The United States Embassy in Brussels urged Americans "to shelter in place and remain at home." A statement on the embassy website on Saturday advised that "if you must go out, avoid large crowds." The security alert followed the discovery of weapons in the home of a Brussels resident arrested in connection with the

terrorist attacks in Paris on November 13. The weapons were found on Friday in Molenbeek, the heavily immigrant Brussels borough where at least three of the Paris attackers, all Belgium residents from Moroccan immigrant families, had lived. The borough has seen a series of police raids over the past week as the authorities sought to uproot a suspected support network behind the carnage in Paris. Adding to alarm over Belgium's role as a center of Islamic extremism, the Turkish authorities on Saturday arrested a Belgian national of Moroccan ancestry, described as an Islamic State militant, at a luxury hotel in Antalya, along with two others. They identified the Belgian as Ahmad Dahmani, twenty-six, and said he was trying to illegally cross the border into Syria. As the Belgian government's threat analysis unit raised the country's threat level to 4, the highest possible, for the Brussels region, rumors of heavily armed terrorists in a car and bomb threats created a mood of deep foreboding in the city, which is home to not only Belgium's government but also to the headquarters of the European Union and NATO.

—I am not going back to the Brittany, I can assure you.

—The clientele or the . . .

—A mix of toughs and bank managers.

—We'll stick to the Emerald Isle, then, or the Blarney Stone. When do you return?

—Looks like Friday week.

—And then what?

—I've cleared the decks. To Ussy and see if anything stirs in the bramble.

—*Godot* and the novels keep doing well, at Grove at least.

—I may be spent at last!

In Germany, Beckett wanted to see modern paintings and sculpture, abstract and expressionist, and had to hunt them out and finagle introductions and permissions to gain access. He wanted to meet artists and collectors—he was not there to buy but to look. During this time, Hitler and his minister of culture, Joseph Goebbels, were orchestrating an assault on artistic expression and they did so with relish, even staging a major art show of work designated as "degenerate art" (*Entartente Kunst*) that toured the country for three years. Paintings were burned, paintings were auctioned off; artists were "shamed"; supporters of the wrong kind of art lost jobs. Beckett tried to buy a monograph on a sculptor he admired, Ernst Barlach, but the book had been banned, copies confiscated. Ever persistent, Beckett tried to buy a copy directly from the publisher, whom he phoned. Reinhard Piper told his caller that it was not possible to fulfill the order and said so, according to Beckett, in a "very terrified tone." From October 2, 1936, to April 2, 1937, twenty-six weeks, Beckett traveled throughout Germany— Hamburg, Lübeck, Luneburg, Hannover, Brunswick, Wolfenbüttel, Hildesheim, Berlin, Halle, Weimar, Erfurt, Naumburg, Leipzig, Dresden, Freiburg, Bamberg, Staffelstein, Ban, Würzburg, Nürnberg, Regensburg, Munich—looking at, looking for, art. Consider the nerviness of this. Beckett, alone, was in a place where art was dangerous, where art, however degraded, mattered, livelihoods and lives in the balance. He was a demanding critic who knew what he was looking for: he condemned the work of one painter for the sin of having perspective in the painting—"the optical experience post rem, a hideous inversion of the visual process, the eye waiving its privilege," he said of Max Klinger.

But I cannot trust a stranger with my stories, much less an impostor. And that's where literature comes in, the standard trove. To my "love" I give Scheherazade's "The City of Brass":

The grandees and officers of the Khallif Abboulmelik ben Merwan tell him how King Solomon used to confine Jinn in copper vessels by stopping them with lead sealed with his signet. Talib ben Sehl speaks of a place in Africa where such vessels are frequently found, and the khalif sends him for some, together with Abdulaziz ben Merrwan, the governor of Cairo, the khalif's own brother. An old sheikh, Abdussemed, son of Abdulcuddous es Semoudi, serves as guide, and the journey requires two years. The expedition, astray in a desert, arrives at a gruesome, high castle of black stone, surrounded by a thousand steps, with a door of gleaming China steel and a dome of lead. This is recognized as a landmark on the way to the City of Brass, which in turn is but two months from their destination. The walls are inscribed with verses telling the vicissitudes of fortune and

*the passing of glory into dust. "The world," one
reads, "is like unto the vain dreams of the dreamer,
the mirage of the desert which the thirsty take for
water; and Satan maketh it fair for men even unto
death." The writer's kingly majesty and happiness
were obliterated, the verses declare, by a plague
that smote his city and which neither his army nor
his wealth could stay. Continuing, the expedition
reaches a horseman of brass on a high hill, who,
when his hand is rubbed, revolves and points
the way.*

Belgian Prime Minister Charles Michel said on Saturday
that the threat level had been raised because of
"information, relatively precise, of a risk of an attack
similar to the one that unfolded in Paris." Potential
targets included commercial centers, public transport,
shopping streets, and large public gatherings, Mr.
Michel said. "We recommend to the people to respect
all safety instructions and to stay informed via official
announcements," he added, advising people to discount
a fog of rumors and unconfirmed reports. A railway
station under the headquarters of the European Union's
executive offices was sealed off early Saturday and all
traffic on the Brussels metro system was stopped.

—The seats I find hard.
　　—With nothing to lance, I won't complain.
　　—A refreshment?
　　—It's Friday; why not. Out to East Hampton for
the weekend?
　　—Barney and Christine are there already, but

I'm staying on at Houston Street, with Alan. Sidney and I are going to the Frick and the Modern Art Sunday morning. Joe Coffey's taking us 'round in his Morgan.

Beckett's German sojourn began in the northern port city of Hamburg on the second of October 1936, he having arrived via boat from Cork. He read Celine's *Mort à crédit* on the passage. Hamburg offered him artists—their work and their selves. He met and liked painters Karl Kluth and Willem Grimm, Karl Ballmer, and Eduard Bargheer, a man he described as "appallingly alive and possessed." He was shown around Hamburg's art world by, it seems, a covey of women, ranging from a schoolmistress and several widows to a woman who apparently had little interest in the Irishman with a herpes sore on his lip. Still, Beckett enjoyed Hamburg, its churches and cemeteries, but mostly the art. He was impressed by the works of Edvard Munch and Emil Nolde. He wrote dutifully each night about what he had seen during the day.

They come to a brazen pillar containing, sunken to his armpits, an Afrit that had been the demon within the idol of a king who once defied Solomon. The king having been defeated in a prodigious battle—involving armies of birds, serpents, beasts, and Jinn—his Afrit had been sealed in this column to the Day of Judgment. He miserably points the way to the City of Brass, and the company moves on. Then they behold its walls, which are of black

stone, with two towers of Andalusian brass that
gleam from a distance like fires. A man sent around
on a camel takes three days and finds the wall
one block. They climb a hill and gaze down into
the city, descrying lofty palaces, domes glittering,
running streams, orchards, and flowering
pleasances; but all is still, save for the hooting of
the owl in the markets, the wheeling of birds above
the gardens, and the croak of ravens in the streets.
Inscriptions on the walls warn of the vanities of
time. A ladder is constructed and a man mounts.
When he reaches the top he stares, then claps his
hands, crying out, "By Allah, thou art fair!" casts
himself into the city, and is dashed to pieces.

A police hotline for information about his whereabouts
has received hundreds of calls but none have provided the
authorities with enough information. The Belgian news
media has speculated that he may be dead. Mr. Dahmani,
the Belgian national arrested in Turkey on his way to
Syria, is suspected of having been "in contact with the
terrorists who perpetrated the Paris attacks," said a Turkish
official who spoke on condition of anonymity, in line with
government protocol. He arrived in Turkey from Amsterdam
on November 14 — the day after the Paris attacks.

—No, the Guggenheim Museum was enough. An
hour there was *more* than enough. Peggy has all the
good stuff.

—Have you been to Venice? You should go, not to
die . . .

—No. I sent Suzanne for the opening of *Oh les*

98

beaux jours at the festival there—and well-received it was. But no, I don't walk on water.

"Nolde's *Christus and Kinder*, clot of yellow infants, long green back of Christ (David?) leading to black and beards of Apostles. Lovely eyes of child held in His arms. Feel at once on terms with the picture, and that I want to spend a long time before it, and play it over and over again like the record of a quartet." As winter came on, Beckett, with a festering finger and a most inconveniently located boil ("between wind and water"), moved from Hamburg to Berlin, where his experience darkened with the century's. This is where the "trip" became "a failure." But also where he met a young bookseller, Axel Kaun, in letters to whom he famously articulated his aesthetic.

Eleven others do the same. Finally the old Sheikh Abdussemed, committing himself to Allah, ascends and gazes likewise, while all fear for him, but he turns and cries, "Have no fear, for God hath averted me from the wiles and malice of Satan." What he had seemed to see were ten beautiful maidens beckoning, and below, a lake; but when he bethought himself, this illusion disappeared. Doubtless it was an enchantment devised by the people of the city. Walking to the towers of brass, the sheikh discovers two gates of gold without visible opening, but a brazen horseman carries in his outstretched hand a notice to turn twelve times the pin in his navel. This done, the gates open with a noise of thunder.

"There is no record of the Belgian authorities having warned Turkey about Dahmani—which is why there was no entry ban," the official said. He added: "Had the Belgian authorities alerted us in due time, Dahmani could have been apprehended at the airport."

—This is actually very pleasant, Dick. It is nice that the field empties between changing sides. For a moment, we are all looking at an open meadow.

To Axel Kaun: "It is to be hoped the time will come, thank God, in some circles it already has, when language is best used where it is most efficiently abused. Since we cannot dismiss it all at once, at least we do not want to leave anything undone that may contribute to its disrepute. To drill one hole after another into it until that which lurks behind, be it something or nothing, starts seeping through—I cannot imagine a higher goal for today's writer."

The sheikh finds in the guard room men sitting dead but wearing keys, with which he opens the principal gate, whereupon those of the expedition, crying "god is most great!" go into the silent city. The inhabitants are sitting in their shops and homes with shriveled skin and rotted bones; the markets are sumptuous with silks and pearls; the palace is magnificent. Tablets admonish of the passing of the glories of the world.

VLADIMIR: One of the thieves was saved. (*Pause.*)

It's a reasonable percentage. (*Pause.*) Gogo.

—But I could do without the bloody organ.

Beckett's aesthetic of failure was born in German cities that would be bombed to smithereens during the next eight or nine years—it is where he may have begun to "[fix] an existence on the threshold of solution," as Nixon surmises in the last line of his book on the *German Diaries*, quoting Beckett in a letter to Simone de Beauvoir.

Visiting the various rich pavilions, the company carries off as much wealth as it can.

ESTRAGON: What?

VIII.

—This Houston team is most cooperative, soft taps around the pitch, or the infield, is it?

It was not easy for Beckett to fail at writing.

And they see in the palace, on a great couch, a fair damsel, embalmed with exceeding art, guarded by two slaves—a white having a mace and a black with a sword—between whom stands a tablet recounting the past glories of the kings of the world and naming the damsel, Tedmureh, daughter of the Kings of the Amalekites; seven successive years of drought had destroyed her realm.

I was ten years old when the towers fell downtown, about a mile from my school.

—It's like a game of pepper.
—You'll have to translate. *Et pas en Francais.*

I mean to say it was hard for him to fail. He was a brilliant linguist, named a lecturer in French at Trinity College at age twenty-four; he wrote works and thousands of letters in English, French, and

German to friends, publishers, theater people, and could also speak Italian, Spanish, and Portuguese; he could read music. Beckett was so gifted it was up to him to sabotage his own scholarly career, and he did—after publishing a brilliant book on Proust, he left the academy behind, deeply disappointing his mentor at Trinity—and his mother.

"When," the text makes known, "we despaired of succor, we displayed all our riches and things of price and, shutting the gates of the city, resigned ourselves to the judgment of our Lord and committed our affair to our Master. Know, O though who comest to this place, that she whom thou seest here was not deluded by the world and its frail delights." The governor of Cairo begins making copies of all the tablets and loading as much as possible on his camel.

Our teacher, Susan, was talking about our big trip that year, to Williamsburg, when the principal came in, Phil. It was a nice day, real blue out, and all of us were still in our summer mode and *so* not into school and homework.

—Pepper. It's a game, my father taught me, more of a drill, where balls are tossed from a short distance, less than the distance here, which is sixty feet six inches, by the way, twenty meters or so, and the batter is meant to just make contact, just hit it, a controlled tap back to the pitcher or some other fielder surrounding him. It's meant to sharpen the batter's eye, and coordination.

—The other side's good at that game.

—Too bad for them [*laughing*] it's not the sport.

—Perhaps these two squads should form their own association. Head-and-head.

Beckett's mind was suffused with literary forms, styles, cadences. To escape tradition, he had to leave his native language, English, for the language of his adopted country, French, in order to get away from any inherited literary "style." Name an important writer who has made such a move for such a reason; name a writer, regardless of importance, who has made such a move for such a reason. Well, you probably cannot. No doubt his lucky apprenticeship with James Joyce (who spoke eleven languages and took on literary styles only to then shred them) daubed Beckett thickly with ambition, certainly with an understanding that an artist could—should—abandon tradition to find what was new and necessary. Beckett, like Joyce, was a modernist. Perhaps the last, as biographer Anthony Cronin argues.

Talib ben Sehl, on the other hand, ascends to take the jewels from the damsel, the white mace-bearer smites his back, and the black swordsman cuts off his head. "May God," says the governor, "have no mercy on thy soul! Indeed, there was enough in these treasuries, and to covet assuredly dishonor a man." All depart, and they shut the gates as before. The expedition comes to a nation of blacks that are true believers, having been taught by

a man that came out of the sea, from whom a
light issued that illumined the whole horizon.
The king of these people sends out divers, who
return with twelve vessels sealed with Solomon's
seal, as well as several mermaids, whereafter the
company, having achieved their purpose, return to
Damascus.

Phil and Susan talked out in the hall. I saw Susan put her hand over her mouth and look at Phil like he had said something awful. We figured we'd find out soon enough, even too soon, so Henry and I tossed his hacky sack back and forth while one of the girls looked at us weird. Zack took out his *Sports Illustrated.* Oliver slipped about five sticks of gum into his mouth. Then Susan came back in, her lips pressed tight, looking at us, sort of, but over our heads, out the window. This is how she looked when she was what she called flummoxed, looking for an answer to something, like when she found the trash basket half full of milk and a couple of pencils floating there, yesterday.

—For crissakes, a late rally. That ball's fair. Christopher into second!
    —We're awake.
    —Just wait. . . . Pitching change.
    —A new bowler at last. Long innings. That organist, for fuck's sake!

Did Beckett "fail better," as he wished? Did he drill holes in the language, as he said a contemporary writer must, and if he did, what seeped through? Is it Being? *Back unsay shades can go. Go and come*

*again. No. Shades cannot go. Much less come
again. Nor bowed old woman's back. . . .*

*The khalif opens the vessels one by one. Devils
emerge, crying, "We repent, O prophet of God!"
and the khalif marvels at the power of Solomon.
Tanks are constructed for the mermaids, but they
die of the heat. The khalif divides the spoils of the
City of Brass among the faithful. And the governor,
bestowing his office on his son, goes to Jerusalem,
to worship God, where he remains till his death.
This, then, is all that has come down to us of the
story of the City of Brass.*

I say to her this tale. She feigns sleep. But I am an
impostor, too, poured in brass.

Then she started to talk and just as she was getting
our attention we couldn't hear what she was saying.
There were sirens blaring and the big honk that fire
trucks make when they are trying to move traffic out
of the way. She walked in a trot, then she slowed down,
over to the window, and tried to close it, still talking.
She was talking about a thing that had happened that
involved us having to get back to school work. I pocketed
Henry's hacky sack, and we welcomed what seemed like
a little break in our discussion of colonial America. But
then Phil came back in, with the headmaster next to
him, and they spoke to Susan with their hands out, as
if saying, "Stay." So we stayed. Susan said she would be
right back. She asked us all to read the Magna Carta in
our books.

—You see, smart move. Woodeshick calmed the waters. And Frank Thomas is a tough man to get out. Three strikes.

—[*Drawing out the syllables*] Woodeshick?

—Not that kid coming up . . . Hickman now. Maybe our best player.

—A replacement?

—Pinch hitter we call it.

—No one to catch that on the fly!

—Runs scores. Now two-zip, Mets.

—An obscene margin!

. . . Nor old man and child. Nor foreskull and stare. Blur yes. Shades can blur. When stare clamped to one alone. Or somehow words again. Go no nor come again. Till dim if ever go. Never to come again. Blanks for when words gone. When nohow on. Then all seen as only then.

Will fiction keep the truth at bay or usher it forth? Does truth usher forth fiction or keep it at bay? Are these two real questions or two fictive ones? Or one of each, and if so, which is which? Are these propositions exhaustive of all possibilities? No. Truth, say, might both usher fiction forth and keep it at bay. Similarly, fiction might do the same to truth. The twilight of delusion, perhaps. Dreams of truth. I am dead, no one knows it. I am here, same deal, same dead.

I raised my hand—I think I did—and told her I'd left my textbook at home and she didn't even see me. So we all, most of us anyway, just fooled around for ten minutes or so. Then Susan came back and we read the Magna Carta—or she did—out loud. But Maria's mom showed up and talked to Susan near the door and then left with Maria. Then Vio's dad came, and then we realized something was up, like a big fire or something. Phil showed up again and addressed the class. His shirt sleeves were rolled but he was very calm, except he rubbed his hands together more than usual, like he was washing them. I don't remember what Phil said. Oliver's father, Andrew, showed up in a sharp suit—he's in the music business—and he took charge and told me I was going back with them, that he'd call Mom and Dad. He said the World Trade Center had been hit by two planes. I couldn't wait to see what this was about, but when we got to the lobby of the school, I got scared. Parents and kids were mixed in there and it was as if everyone wanted to rush out but wanted to stay, like they didn't know what to do.

—Stengel is letting the pitcher bat. The Old Professor.

—God, not an academic running things. . . .

—They call him the professor, because he talks in circles.

—It's that simple? Professor . . . Stengel?

—He was a genius, when he managed great players, with the Yankees, not that long ago.

—There was a Professor Stengel married a great Polish soprano.

—No relation, I'm sure, Casey's from Kansas City, hence Kay-Cee."

While visiting his mother in Dublin after the war, Beckett had a "revelation" (his word), an experience recounted poetically if cryptically in *Krapp's Last Tape*: " . . . that memorable night in March, at the end of the jetty, in the howling wind, never to be forgotten, when suddenly I saw the whole thing. . . . [C]lear to me at last that the dark I have always struggled to keep under is in reality my most— unshatterable association until my dissolution of storm and night with the light of the understanding and the fire." Beckett was forty and had already published his stories, several poems, and the novel *Murphy*. In short order he would go on to compose the postwar works that have made him such a large figure, but one need look only at chapter 6 in *Murphy*, finished years before, in 1935, to see that his revelation was of a reality already within him, at a deep level, the third of "three zones," of which Murphy was conscious, it appears, and so, we may assume, was Beckett. He describes "Murphy's Mind" thus: "The third, the dark [zone], was a flux of forms, a perpetual coming together and falling asunder of forms. The light contained the docile elements of a new manifold, the world of the body broken up into the pieces of a toy; the half light, states of peace. . . . [N]othing but forms becoming and crumbling into fragments of a new becoming, without love or hate or any intelligible principle of change. Here there was nothing but commotion and the pure forms of commotion. Here he was not free, but a mote in the dark of absolute freedom."

In the dark. In the dusk. In the wake. In the gloaming. All is seen, in the dark, in the dusk, in the wake, in the gloaming. In the dark. In the dusk. In the wake. In the gloaming.

Andrew seemed like he knew what to do, but that was reassuring only for a minute, because he greeted every other parent with a serious shake of the head, in a very disapproving way. When we got to the sidewalk, we could sense something really bad had happened. Sirens were screaming. Traffic on Sixth Avenue was clogged. And to our left, there were the towers, both with dark gray smoke pouring out of them, like they were on fire. Getting across town on foot wasn't easy. There was not only the traffic, but people walking uptown, half-running. It was as crowded as on Halloween, when the parade goes through and people come from all over to see it. When we got to Seventh Avenue, all the cars were gone.

—And the pitcher hits! That's in. Three to nothing.

—Insurmountable, if recent events are any judge.

—Have you heard any music here? It's a good jazz town.

Beckett's "vision at last," reported variously to have occurred on the East pier in Dún Laoghaire (by Eoin O'Brien) and "my mother's room" (Beckett himself, to Knowlson), was perhaps there all along. But this vision or revelation is a sort that is worn as a burden—all these tumbling forms ("great granite rocks the foam flying up in the light of the lighthouse and the wind-gauge spinning like a propeller," from *Krapp*) constituting "the dark of absolute freedom" (*Murphy*) demand a certain posture toward self and expression. Beckett put it perfectly in *Murphy*, of Murphy: "Here he was not free. . . . He did not move, he was a point in the ceaseless unconditioned generation and passing away of line." That is, "you must go on, I can't go, I'll go on"—the formulation that draws to a close *The Unnamable*, twenty years later in a changed world, a postwar world, but still a Beckett world. The question of Being's relationship to form continues as central to his practice.

Nothing is seen, in the dark, in the dusk, in the wake, in the gloaming. What is seen is the dark. The dusk. The wake. The gloaming.

We could look all the way to our right, uptown, toward St. Vincent's—no cars. But there were beds, like stretchers, out front of the hospital, right in the street. But looking downtown, down Seventh Avenue, there was a wall of people coming toward us, like out of a horror movie. There was smoke behind them, there was smoke coming off them. They were gray like they were dead.

—Jazz . . . ? Only at Barney's, in his Quonset hut out there. On the phonograph. I take to my room.

Eventually, Beckett's formulations embraced failure, more importantly, the *sustaining* of failure (going on), as a goal. Sustaining failure is the art of living— this is Beckett's key philosophical, biological, and literary insight—facing failure and not surrendering to its darkness. "I see my light dying," says Clov rather defiantly to the unsighted Hamm when asked why he is staring at the wall.

These appalling reductions! What remains? Give me the remainder.

When we got to Oliver's apartment in the Archive Building, near the river, we went into his room and took two Cokes with us. Oliver had some cool things, so this was okay. It seemed strange to be there during the day, though—with his father all dressed up and on the phone in the kitchen.

—Let's see if the home team can close this out.

Is this what makes us lovable?

What's the remainder?

I wondered where my parents were.

.

IX.

—That fellow's very deft.

> For Beckett, the high priest of failure—"fail better,"
> "like none other dare fail," "better worse," "say
> nohow on"—what are we to make of the works he
> abandoned?

The remainder is comedy.

> After we played a few games—we shot baskets into his
> hoop, fooled around online, and then played with his
> remote-control cars, we got on his bed and looked out
> his window, which had a view from high up of the Hudson
> River and the highway that runs along it.

—Roy McMillan. One of the best at his position.
  —Hoovers everything up.
  —One out to go.

> Did Beckett's abandoned work, of which there are
> a dozen or so—abandoned plays, radio scripts,
> essays, poems, translations, and a few prose
> pieces—not fail enough? Did they fail the test of
> failure? Else why abandoned? Did they edge

toward success, or some facile form of failure, or were they abandoned because their ambitions for failure were too grand, the failure envisioned unattainable or the execution too poorly conceived?

What's left over is comedy. It is strictly human. Henri Bergson said that.

Coming down the highway were nothing but EMS vehicles and fire trucks. We turned on the TV and had trouble finding a station that was working but then found CNN and we sat watching. I got butterflies in my stomach.

—So what do you make of this filmmaking, Sam?
—The *movie* part of it. The camera moving, the eye. It changes possibilities. Narrator on a dolly.
—Next stop, Hollywood!

Or were there landscapes of failure that Beckett considered too dark to traverse, prompting retreat? An afternoon in the Beckett archive at the University of Reading reading the six pages of his abandoned prose work "Long Observation of the Ray," from 1976, written in English in his small, slanted hand and a series of typewritten drafts, suggests to me that there is indeed a place too dark for Beckett. This elaborately schemed piece—meant to cover nine "themes" in precise mathematically determined packets of sentences, with a structure described by Steven Connor, one of only two scholars who have written on "Long Observation," as proceeding in "exactly equivalent increment(s)

116

and diminishment(s), consisting of one sentence referring to each" of the nine themes . . . followed by "a sequence of three sentences referring to" the nine themes, "followed by similar sequence of six, nine, six and three sentences," concluding with another sequence of one sentence each "from the nine themes," was worked on by Beckett for over the span of a year before being dropped. "Long Observation of the Ray" attempts to describe the play of light (from a lantern) within a hermetic spherical chamber six feet in diameter, and how the light can be made to wash with equal intensity the entire surface from an identical distance, which is required for the intensity to remain constant. Beckett encounters and fiddles with many of the epistemological and technical problems this scheme presents. He is trying to hold constant a closed system with the light source not biasing what it illuminates. The second essay on this mysterious piece, by David Houston-Jones, hints at a possible reason.

"An animal which laughs," Bergson said, of us. The comic occurs in the absence of feeling, Bergson said. "Laughter has no greater foe than emotion," he said. But laughter has a social function—it "stands in need of an echo." *We don't manage too badly, eh Didi, between the two of us?*

Andrew came in. Oliver and I chewed gum. Dad showed up. Dad talked to Andrew for a while and then Dad asked Andrew if he had any whiskey. Andrew did, and Dad soon had a glass in his hand.

—I wrote Jackie a note. Not an idea in my head but I can see something . . . with Jackie MacGowran in it.

—Jack's been very busy, hasn't he?

—Yes, blessedly. He's a danger to himself at all times, but when idle, it worsens. He despairs.

—He's one of the best. He couldn't do *Film*?

—Just too many commitments, I'd have loved it, but I'd have been sent home in a box.

"Beckett's later work," writes Houston-Jones, "is preoccupied with a world running down to zero." Beckett's interest is in "what survives the disappearance of the human species." The work is "rooted" in William Thompson's formulation of the Second Law of Thermodynamics, according to which energy in a closed system is gradually lost, resulting in stabilization at absolute zero. Beckett's abandoned piece, Houston-Jones proposes, emerges as a picture of "human survival in informational form." This is Beckett perhaps trying to design an object that can realize in some fashion James Maxwell's thought experiment, in which the Second Law is refuted by having a door through which slowing and therefore cooling particles can be exchanged for accelerating and therefore warming particles within, keeping energy constant. Beckett's sphere and lantern and ray arguably have a go at this. But given the concerns of the late Beckett work, I might side with Steven Connor who sees "Long Observation" as Beckett's attempt to remove the theatrical from art, and from theater, to purify its abstraction. To get at what? Toward being? The shape of being?

I said to her, tell me a joke. I said to her, make it funny. I said to her, let's be light, the light in our future. The light ahead. I said to her, you see it, don't you? Close your eyes, you will see it. I said to her, if you can see it, tell me about it. Be my echo, I will hear it, you back to me. You back to me.

It was still morning. I always thought drinking was something grownups did to celebrate, like New Year's or a birthday, not the collapse of buildings or whatever this was. They were calling it a terrorist act on TV. America had been attacked. Maybe you did drink to that. Dad borrowed Andrew's cell phone because he had to make some calls, he said, and Andrew was on the land line. I had to help Dad work the cell, since he was bad at technology. I wondered if most adults were drinking somewhere.

—The camera destroys space. It invades it. Radio makes it disappear, but the camera moves through it.
    —And can recreate it, wouldn't you say. *Potemkin*?
    —Constitutes it somehow. Moving collage. Montage. Take space and ravage it and then put it on a wall, on a screen. The possibilities are not endless, but far beyond the stage set.
    —Liberating?

From the unpublished "Long Observation of the Ray":

More than with the weakness itself the struggle is with the constant degree of weakness. Latent early this adversary could not fully emerge till late. Before the mind even weaker then than before and knowing it. Weakened by struggle with other adversaries earlier to emerge. The eye strains henceforward for greater weakness however little or less. And so perhaps fails to see what but for this preoccupation it might have seen.

So faint that in less utter darkness it might pass unseen it grows no fainter! Colourless no trace of yellow white faint white. Ashen waver through the air ending in ashen blur. Jaggedness as though the dark opaque in patches. Whether faintness due to that of inexhaustible source. Or to nursing some finite blaze.

Make it funny, you said. Let's be light, you said. The light in our future. You make me Narcissus. Narcissus, you say. Tell me a story, we say. Tell me about the dog that ran away. Tell me about the family dog that ran away, that ran away. Ha-ha-ha how to write laughter. You can't write laughter you can only run away. You ran away. I fell for it.

Dad took me home. On the way, Dad got money out of the ATM on Christopher Street, which took quite a while. Dad seemed proud of himself to have thought of getting some cash, like the banks were gonna run out. Then we went

120

to our apartment, where Dad got on the phone again. He reached Mom, who was on her way—on foot, to get Alison up at Dalton. We watched TV for the rest of the day. We ate spaghetti that night. The Yankee game was canceled. After dinner we watched *O Brother, Where Art Thou?* in the den, although Dad and Mom went to the kitchen a lot. Mom drank a lot of wine; Dad drank beer. They had the radio on in there.

—I wouldn't go that far. Haven't you read your Sartre? Come now . . .
    —*Mais oui.*
    —It's a figment, Dick.
    —Freedom, you mean?
    —Mean? Let's stick to the match. That man is bowling fast.

How else explain the fluctuant structure and pulse of "Long Observation of the Ray"—that regular increase and decrease in the size of sentence units equally distributed across a set of nine themes, a kind of metabolic rhythm approaching a steady-state—than to say it is intended as a model for eternal being, at whatever the cost. That is, not an accretive narrative that resolves itself, not at all; and not a system that winds itself down to an end; but a sort of machine, with its intensities, exposures, and frequencies set in such a way as to pertain forever, defeating entropy. Is this what failed Beckett, this machine he had built? Or did the prospect of its *succeeding* horrify him? Endless system survival, a horror show? I don't know. David Houston-Jones called the abandoned work, its mere six pages, "a monument to extinction." But I believe Beckett said no to this once he faced it. A monument to extinction Beckett never built, even if he'd drawn up the plan. But this is provisional.

I said to her, it doesn't matter, whether we are interred or burned or buried at sea. Light is our future. Rising. Show me the light, tell us of the light, I said to her. I said to her, my beloved, we've only so many sentences left, we might start to savor them a little bit, conserve, conserve. Suddenly—no!—at last, at long last, you begin to speak. You are good at this. Go on. Change my tune.

I went to bed late, knowing school was canceled for the next day. Nothing was moving, no work for the grownups. In the morning, Dad had to run—I mean jog—up to 14th Street to find a newspaper. "US ATTACKED" it said on the front page of the *Times*. Dad said, "Nothing will ever be the same." So did Mom. So did everyone, so I guess they knew. The next day, everyone was on the phone all day. The city had a horrible smell.

—Pop to shortstop! That should do it. Macmillan . . . game over, Mets win.

—[*Clapping*] No ninth try for the . . . Metropolitans?

—The home team doesn't bat if it's ahead in the ninth inning.

—A mercy.

For the record, the nine themes: observation, chamber, inlet-outlet, constant intensity (inexhaustible source), faintness, cross-section (lantern), constant length, saltatoriality, extinction-occultation. The noun "saltatoriality" is not a word, though Beckett glossed it as "erratic transfer from one blank to another." "Saltatorially" *is* a word, an adverb, describing how active processes are ensured in sodium channels in the nervous system. Had Beckett's narrative interest brought him here, to neuronal salt transfers? These are dark workings indeed, in which the "Long Observation of the Ray" takes place within a spherical chamber with an inner light source of no dimension. And yet none of this can be seen, as the sphere is closed.

Someone said, you cannot stay here. None could stay there and could not continue. Describe the site, it is not important. A flat plain, then a mountain, no, a hill, wild, so wild. Enough. The summit a kind of marsh, with heath to the knee, sheep paths, mud tracks, my life, a scribble, a scramble barely visible, ruts deepened by rains, effaced by rains.

Dad always said I had a great nose for smells and for describing them. Tar and floor polish for the skunk smell in Connecticut. That was a good one. For the Ground Zero smell—they were calling it ground zero—it was harder. I tried but I'd never smelled these smells before, except maybe for a wet campfire like we made once in the Adirondacks. But it also smelled like when Oliver and I once lit a plastic straw with a match.

—Curtain, then. Now what, Dick?

—There's a second act, game two, in about twenty minutes. So what do you think?

Traffic is slow. Traffic is stop and go. Be prepared to stop.

Or best not to stay the wanderer even if. Worse yet to wander on, even if. For better or worse, wander on.

At the bottom of one of these I was lying, out of the wind. Couldn't see shit, didn't want to—the valleys, distant lakes like blue coins out there, the sea on its shelf. I should not have begun so, but as it goes, I had to start.

We weren't supposed to go outside much, because of the air. And lots of people thought there might be follow-up attacks, since they couldn't tell how many "cells" were in the country. It was like they were talking about a sickness.

—[*Lighting a small cigar*] We'll stay on.

Be prepared to go.

Someone said so, perhaps the same person who made you come.

Everywhere looking for cells.

PART TWO

I.

The other window.

All the same, so as not to have entered the room with trepidation, I might have reminded myself that there were various old friends of my family who bore the same sophistication as the Greenes; companions of my early days who were just as fond of the arts, and, as well, as fond of those who patronized the arts; but I did not.

The *other* window. I meant the other window. The *other* window.

If indeed I had fortified my confidence by recollection of former acquaintances of some artistic taste and standing, I might have entered the rooms with a swagger and not the hunched terror of one about to be sentenced, or summarily lashed; consequently, I would not have ventured, by way of introducing myself, a word game. Feigning, by dint of a studied distraction, to have arrived at the Greenes already far along in some intricate chain of calculations, I condescended to share my exploratory musings, having come down to earth, as it were. "I am trying to determine the most beautiful and pleasing two-word phrase in the English language, just now, and I am quite sure I have found it," I announced, tricking my eyes to brim brightly and quiver at the lids, as if intellectual jet fuel were still sloshing in my tanks.

> No. The other window. Not that one, not this one or that other one. Yes, the other window. That one. The other one.

"Autumn sunlight," I offered. This was received in such a manner as would be the announcement of my name, with which there is nothing to quibble or even judge, since we were not, say, at a salon of high snobbery, such as the Verdurins'. Still, a tough crowd. "Autumn," I went on, undaunted, as proudly as if explaining my home province. Being inherently diachronic, one in a familiar series of terms defined by *tempus*, and, of course, as it comes in the wake of summer's cooling and antecedent to winter's icy chill, "autumn" is capable of a warm welcome in most rooms, so I tried. "It is resplendent," I glossed, repeating the entire phrase, "with a mixture of tones and colors, of different temperatures, like, say 'sea-green dress.'"

> Sam, where shall I look while I'm rocking? Where. Shall. I. Look? Inward, he said. Billie Whitelaw tells us this. Look through the other window. The other window is inward.

"Autumn sunlight," I went on, "chills with its warmth, such as when, after a swim in a cold mountain lake, one stretches upon the sunbaked basalt of the shore and shivers." I immediately regretted the false intonation, the artificial sonority of my own voice and hints of tourism, whereas I would have done just as well, perhaps even better, to abandon myself to invective rather than strive for the touch of Wordsworth. I understood in a painful instant that there was probably not, in the whole of the Greene circle, even one of the "faithful" who loved me, or believed in me, as dearly as I did love and believe in myself. I don't mean belief in the sense of an acolyte to his God but, say, as a gambler to his play in the fifth at Chantilly. Of course I did favor myself, no matter the field, for I was raised well. So, despite committing my missteps barely past the threshold of the Greenes, before any refreshment taken or formal introductions hazarded, I kept swinging, as my father most heartily advised no matter the occasion, as if life could be counted upon, like a mechanical pitching arm, to autonomically hurl opportunities toward the plate, and you there, bat in hand while at bat you were, beholden only to stand in and "take a rip." My word game having dribbled to little notice on the carpet, I determined to express yet another sentiment. But first, for preparation is not a foolish habit, I assessed the room, and there I saw the painter, the pianist, the host and hostess and their charming daughter. This quintet arrayed before me—oh, to be mired in a metaphor—like an infield, is what I came for, why I was there, why I am anywhere, looking for art and family.

Sit at the window, the other window. When the skies are clear she sees Venus rise. Followed by the sun. At evening, at the other window, rigid in her old spindle-backed chair, when the skies are clear, she sees Venus emerge from the growing dark before it, too, disappears into the gloom. She sits on in her own deepening dark. For what purpose.

There was that change in atmospheric pressure, like the wind dropping to gather itself elsewhere, or for another go at a spent willow; a break in intentionality that is either a brief respite or a permanent rescue, time will tell. And indeed, we moved on—that is to say, I was absorbed, as a socius, into the sodality of the room, and I could breathe. A respite, at least, I would wager, but no rescue: offered a drink from a passing salver, a silly concoction called a Sayonara, favored by the host in favor of the artist, I am told, and, as a guest, one has no choice but to indulge in the sponsor's enthusiasm, and therefore, after extracting the miniature paper coolie hat, I quaffed the saccharine cocktail. Presently, hard upon me, was the artist, swirling his Sayanora like Grace Kelly her martini in *Rear Window*, nervously, conspiratorially, flirtatiously, one Peter Swan, best described thus: long face, a pate fibered like a kiwi, not regularly good-looking altogether but exuding an intelligence; a thin sprawl of fine fuzz across the cheek also, eyeglasses glinting over tired eyes that slouch toward the orbital as in those bad portraits found on velvet in thrift shops, and that smile, meant to make you weep—if you were a six-year-old. But the rheumy eyes are sizing me, and I see his mandibles twitch, as if eager to begin the slow, deadly efficient ingestion of plankton.

Some version of this we read, in university rooms, a small group, a shred of text. Four walls, twelve windows, but one I chose. I read my portion, over and over as directed—"the other window."

I stumbled again, boldly asking if he were any relation to a one-time ballplayer named Swan. At once, Peter Swan looked with amused astonishment, over his right shoulder, toward an invisible third, whom he seemed to call to witness that he had never, in fact, authorized such an inquiry into relations. "Oh, aren't you on a roll," he said, his gaze returned to me with a nearly audible click.

At another window.

"Yes," I said to him—"like butter"—and he flinched ever so slightly, as if I had tapped his kneepad with a hammer.

II.

Where is this place?

My mind was filled with other things, I had a trove of them.

Can there be an inexistent center in a formless place? Can there be other? Can the center be simply the search for an imagined center, the imagined center itself being the search, after Blanchot?

I skipped past His Annoyance as if he were a channel buoy and I only too happy to fulfill his message to steer clear—*Aye-aye!* I headed for deeper waters, toward the host's only daughter, just visible beyond the gleaming black of the piano, she of the long red locks of my imagination and the face of Van Eyck's Mary, oval, sad, resigned. I plotted a course to cheer her, to be taken on board, as it were.

But I am in Antwerp, this day, appearing as fact. My wife is drawing. We are surrounded by 600-year-old buildings, art just as old, and there's old Rubens's house, in a place of perfect May sunshine. Something has happened in this place. Space carved by stone, by water flows, the Scheldt, look. No, the other window.

Despite the current philosophy of the day, in which one's intelligence is understood to increase with the strength of one's *disbelief in everything*, I determined to regale her with my recent reading of Proust, with which, naturally, I was saturated like a biscuit abandoned on a teacup saucer. I quite knew that the following literary anecdote, once unfolded and made manifest for inspection, would charm her, so I proceeded. After an exchange of pleasantries of indescribable banality, I told her of how Marcel considers great art, such as the *petite phrase* of the Vinteuil Sonata, to be something that, before you are exposed to it you are one person and after you are quite another, and remain so, till the end of your time. Proust concludes a gorgeous thought with this: *Et la mort avec elles a quelque chose de moins amer, de moins inglorieux, peut-être de moins probable.* Mademoiselle does not know her Proust very well but does know French, and asks, a puzzled wrinkle through her brow, "*Avec elles*? And death with them? With whom?" And I am ready with the translation. "With beauty, my dear. Here is Moncrieff, in his great Edwardian English: 'And death *in their company* is something less bitter, less inglorious, perhaps even less certain.'"

Inward there is no center. There is no form. There is history but a flash, a mockery of the concept of duration. We teeter on the edge of unbecoming, having just left it, soon to return. This is where we live, not in Antwerp, but in unbecoming, at which we are old hands. What else is here, in this "nonexistent formless place?" Beckett took a long look around. Through the other window. No, the *other* window, to another place, flashes of place, maybe, and measures of music, maybe, or giving on an outer dark.

Milady made to catch her breath! "In their company," she marveled, thinking, marveling more, "death is *perhaps* less certain?" I was delighted at her delight. What an improvement upon the French—"*avec elles*," she scoffed. And further: "*moins probable*, less certain!" I told her directly, closing the space between us, that "in their company" was the key to the intimacy of the entire construction in English. It was not merely an association with the traces, in the mind, of a work of art, but a dialogue with that art, a visitation, which then believably makes—perhaps!—death something other than we had thought. "Yes," she said, with green gaze, "company." Suddenly, no, alas, one long alas, we had some.

Blue sky over the open port, no doubt blue elsewhere, too, that again. Bring the blue sky inward. Can one? What to bring? Bring in no less. Now look around—within, not without.

It was the artist again, now suppressing a cough, or a laugh. He knew his French *and* his Proust, and his hearing was apparently very keen. "Everyone knows that the Scott Moncrieff is outdated, a period piece." But she cut him off with a rapier's glance. "Monsieur and I were talking about *compagnie*, we were not requesting it." *Touché.* And I moved in: "I am interested in Samuel Beckett's use of the word *company* as the title of a most remarkable piece."

To restore silence is the role of objects, Sam said. Restore silence to what, to whom? Tell now.

Je ne suis pas amusant plus un cercle quelconque. I am not amusing, anymore, in any circle. In any company.

Objects may not be silent, but they may be made of silence. They are not even objects, but they may be made of objects.

Yes, I made it to the end, the final volume, where Proust writes *"un livre est un grande cimetière,"* lines underscored by Beckett in his 1929 copy of *Le Temps retrouvé*, volume 2, page 59.

III.

Let's look around, within, not without.

Death of the book, by the book, in the book—*un grande cimetière*—it happens.

Amid emptied spaces, Spartan interiors, vast vacancies, wasted landscapes, bare ruin'd choirs, there are objects, yes. And though characters, such as they are, seeming sentient, may stand mutely before them (unless forced out of silence, by a constable, say, or a playwright), the narrator is far from silent. If you can imagine him speaking.

In the drawing room of the Greenes a heat blast incinerates the assembled, strewn now in heaps, gowns shredded and arms bleeding among the grounded chandeliers, a collapsed piano smoldering like a kiln, one string popping like a shot, another, and you can scratch the air as if it is plaster. Like that. What will accompany our young couple, let's make them young, or will accompany any of us, at that last instant, as we know it, when the dust and nonsense hardens into glass?

Behold the button-hook, weeping.

Of tarnished silver pisciform it hangs by its hook from a nail. It trembles faintly without cease. As if here without cease the earth faintly quaked. The oval handle is wrought to a semblance of scales. The shank a little bent leads up to the hook the eye so far still dry. A lifetime of hooking had lessened its curvature. To the point at certain moments of its seeming unfit for service. Child's play with pliers to restore it.

Schubert accompanied Beckett at the very end, *Der Winterreise*. As did a handful of dear friends, his niece and nephew, his cigars and Irish whiskey, and stretches of recollected poems—Tennyson, Keats, Mallarmé, Yeats. Who was it told me that Yeats gets better as you approach the end, a tattered coat upon a stick? Yes, we might seek company, especially if many have fled, as they do, if we ourselves linger. The twenty-three-year-old Beckett left a trace in black ink in *Du côté de chez Swann* as the narrator rhapsodized about the little phrase of the Vinteuil Sonata: "Like the madeleine, hawthorns, etc. one of the 2 elements — The necessary portentous actual sensation — *of participation*" (my italics). Sixty years later, the dying Beckett was *participating* somehow in Yeats's "The Tower," aware of the clouds fading from sight at nightfall, birdsong approaching silence in the deepening shade—*but the clouds*.

Here, an object is rendered up with a distinct music, an exalted diction, in shapes and letterforms arrayed against a tricky void. This worn silver object, in *Ill Seen*

Ill Said, sits, gorgeous from his hand, against a landscape of stones, like "the stones of Connemara" of Lucky's great monologue, another dolmen. But objects within objects, as inside a rough hovel of language this lovely instrument—a shimmering silver-handled button-hook—hangs. Near the center of an unchartable vastness it shimmers like a thought. A bit of light. When asked—at a dinner party in Dresden—what it is he wanted to create most, a young Beckett replied, "light in the monad." After Leibniz.

Beckett wrote *Company* first in English then in French and then back to English—in truth, it is three works: one for a French reader, from Editions Minuit, a John Calder version for the English reader, and a Grove Press version for the American, with the word-choice differences well mined by Beckett scholars. What was he looking for, wandering from one language to another, gleaning, gathering, sorting—*company*, from the Old French, *compainie*? Toward the end, in his nursing home, Beckett would occasionally borrow a television set on which to watch tennis and rugby. According to James Knowlson, "On one occasion, [Beckett] watched a programme about Bram van Velde, noting with emotion that, as he was being interviewed in a garden, Bram was carrying a copy of Beckett's book, *Compagnie*." What is it about *Company*, the first of three late novellas written in a burst when Beckett was in his seventies, that is so compelling? Perhaps what appears to be straight reminiscences of childhood brings Beckett (the boy) closer to us. J. M. Coetzee describes the prose as "suddenly more expansive, even, by Beckettian standards, genial." Of the fifty-nine paragraphs in *Company*, forty-four of them describe the crawling about of a "dark figure" in a dark landscape who is taken up with "devising" and "imagining"; the other fifteen deal with a male child, walking the Dublin hills with his father, or from the shops with his mother, episodes that, for Coetzee, flicker with "a certain wonder and tenderness." While family relations, often of an estranged nature, alternate, in fugue-like fashion, with a subject split into a voice and a hearer, there is the steady refrain not only of the punning word "lying" but the word *company* itself, which, with its adverbial form, *companionable*, appears thirty-seven times, all done "for company," the entire exercise done for "company in the dark." Is this the "company" of which Proust wrote, the company of art that makes death "less bitter, less inglorious, and perhaps less certain?" It is not fashionable to attribute such a romantic arrangement with death to Beckett, yet Coetzee, again, did not fail to notice a late Beckett letter in which he admits that, even "from the mind in ruins," there is consolation in the thought that "true words at last" may be issued. "To this illusion," wrote Beckett, then seventy-seven, "I continue to cling."

> The world is an infinite set of independent monads, which are indestructible and inimitable. They are in motion, but one monad cannot affect another. There is no causality, everything is pre-established. And all things are "perpetual living mirrors" of every other. This was Gottfried Leibniz's seventeenth-century idea, which impressed the young Beckett, who visited the Leibniz

house in Hannover in 1937. In a letter to MacGreevy, Beckett described Leibniz as "a great cod, but full of splendid little pictures."

If Being is the greatest threat to form, what form does Being deserve? The answer to this question, though it is not so much an answer as a settlement, is arrived at over time, and is coincident, nearly, with the end. Body, mind, social relations, family, are unidirectional and accretive. You are a different person for your history. You have your company. Your *avec elles*.

> To deliver the object, in the light of language, and its colors and sounds, and to do so within one, within an object, within a language, call it a book, is to create and behold. *Behold.* . . . It is the beautiful, pure minimum of what we can do. Note pure, as Beckett said of Schubert's *Rosamunde* Quartet, "pure spirit," an exquisite reduction.

According to John Pilling, as a young man, Beckett, in *Proust*, "must have been gratified to encounter a kindred spirit who had fearlessly pursued the unconventional, and nowhere, perhaps, is this more true than in the matter of what constitutes a person's essential being, which is central to Beckett's work, and is the goal of Proust's also." In *Watt*, a decade after the Proust essay was written, " . . . the inadequacy of language to account for phenomena in the visible world" becomes the principle subject, according to Tom Cousineau. In between these two book-length expressions, Beckett wrote his letter to Axel Kaun, saying that the only thing for a writer to do was to tear a hole in the surface of the language, a kind of violent revolt.

Consider that odd object in *Watt*.

Then we have the septuagenarian, in his final decade, writing his closed-space pieces, and hurtling toward, according to some, a cauterizing literary abstraction but which might be something else—not a simple abstraction, but a putative concreteness, a "nohow on" in a lightless chamber—that Being, that form, that truth. Beckett contradicted this point, in an interview in *Vogue*, of all places, 1970, but I don't believe it: "Perhaps," he said to John Gruen, "like the composer Schonberg or the painter Kandinsky, I have turned toward an abstract language. Unlike them, however, I have tried not to concretise the abstraction. . . . " I think he never stopped trying; he only may have demurred at the notion of having succeeded.

IV.

That odd object in *Watt*.

The blues and the abstract truth.

No, the other object. I mean the other object. The *other*
object.

"Stolen Moments," written in 1960 by Oliver Nelson,
is a sixteen-bar composition derived from blues in
C minor. The tune consists of three melodic ideas, in
eight bars, six bars, two bars, that extend the basic blues
form. For contrast, there are three solos, each twelve
measures in length   by Freddie Hubbard, Eric Dolphy,
and Bill Evans—I count them off, ninety-six beats,
eight to the bar, standing in my kitchen.

Not in *Watt*, *Molloy*. The one that flummoxed me.
Confused I was. It was silver, too, like that other object.
There was little silver in my childhood, very little, mostly
Melmac on our table, plastics. An older world had silver
in it, that older world of silversmiths and tin-knockers.

Let musical ideas, wrote Nelson, determine the form and
shape of the composition. Being, form. Perhaps this work

of mine is not in a literary form, per se, or not solely. Perhaps life is a song, not a story, and has movements, da capo, themes and variations, and perhaps little in the way of narrative drive. "A story is not compulsory, just a life," says the voice in *Texts for Nothing 4*.

Molloy had stolen a little silver from Lousse. One object in his haul eluded my understanding, as to its utility. It had value I was convinced, even if no purpose for it could be discerned, by me. So lovingly described was this object I had never seen that I saw: *"It consisted of two crosses, joined, at their points of intersection, by a bar, and resembled a tiny sawing-horse, with this difference however, that the crosses of the true sawing-horse are not perfect crosses, but truncated at the top, whereas the crosses of the little object I am referring to were perfect, that is to say composed of each of two identical Vs, one upper with its opening above, like all Vs for that matter, and the other lower with its opening below, or more precisely of four rigorously identical Vs, the two I have just named and then two more, one on the right hand, the other on the left, having their openings on the right and left respectively. But perhaps it is out of place to speak here of right and left, of upper and lower. For this little object did not seem to have any base properly so-called, but stood with equal stability on any one of its four bases, and without any change of appearance, which is not true of the sawing-horse. This strange instrument I think I still have somewhere, for I could never bring myself to sell it, even in my worst need, for I could never understand what possible purpose it could serve, nor even contrive the faintest hypothesis on the subject. And from time to time I took it from my pocket and gazed upon it, with an astonished and affectionate gaze . . ."*

If technical facility is a metaphor for comprehensibility, as composer Morton Feldman said, what is comprehensibility a metaphor for? She said she wanted to have an egg this morning. There is only one thing to be done with the request for an egg. Or two, I guess. It is supremely comprehensible. Lyricism without melody, the unmediated contemplation of sound, and the avoidance of dramaticism through the use of understated dynamics, are all evident in Feldman's work. As is the concept of form as a length of time with few divisions or incomprehensible divisions or at best arbitrary ones, such that the piece is kept going without the demands of necessity, thereby either exposing the fallacy that artworks should grow organically or proving that they should. Like various minimal artists, this work rejects the tendency to see the parts as more important than the whole, agreeing with . . . Donald Judd! . . . that, "The thing is to be able to do different things and yet not break up the wholeness that a piece has." That is, to have it all and nothing at all. Nonetheless, the wind still fills the trees for me when I think of god. Tears still fill my eyes when the wind comes around to rally each treetop into harmony with my simple swing of thought, which is more swing than thinking as I swing around and rally as well to a dissolution into something larger, like a voice lost in a choral chant, a note in a symphony, a body absorbed in a crowd. I am the sound I make, a sound incarnate. John Cage, early in his career, extracted essential information about objects by hitting each with the same piece of wood and listening.

What becomes of consciousness at the moment of explosion? Say one explodes one's self, atomizing the body in a concussed flash. What was once arguably an object in a millisecond is radiated in spray and flung viscera, many objects, many fluids, thrown into a suspension of scorched air. Do thoughts and images and words we have known accelerate outward? We handle objects on our tour—ale glasses at the Duvel Historium in Bruges, silver pendants at the gift shop in Ghent—and hear the bomb ticking. In a moment we might be raining in the square.

"To and fro in shadow from inner to outer shadow"—who is it that knows inner shadows from outer shadows? This is the Caravaggio light of Beckett's imagination, life always half in shadow and half in a thin, dying light. Borders, liminalities, crossed and recrossed, "as between two lit refuges whose doors once nearly close, and once turned away from gently part again." You wonder: two lit refuges. Is it this life that is lived between them? Morton Feldman was a natural fit for Beckett since he was the exact opposite artist, a kind of tongue-and-groove orientation. Feldman believed that his material, music, was in itself born perfect and without a history, whereas Beckett, of his material, understood how freighted language was with history, and worked from a disordered and discredited wordshed toward what he hoped, however in vain, might find a more perfect accommodation eventually, knowing that failure, like a friend, awaited him. Feldman asked Beckett for a libretto. He got "Neither" from which "to and fro in shadow" and "two lit refuges" come. Feldman's one-act opera for a single soprano and orchestra sustains an oscillation between things or the idea of things, more accurately a space between sound barriers he's established, where two opposites co-exist, each still a refuge.

> We hole up in our hotel and look out the window not so dark, see the ancient roofs in ranks, the softly stirring treetops, and a distant circus wheel slowly rolling through time. There is no other window, we have only this one window. We perch on the sill and the shouts come up with the birdsong, finches, we think.

Despite Feldman's belief in the perfection of the musical form, he envied a painting's smears, drip, erasures—the painter's touch. "We only have Beethoven's logic," he said.

> Who looks *in* the window?

> *then no sound*
> *then gently light unfading on that unheeded neither*
> *unspeakable home.*

V.

Timelessness in the pauses, eternity.

Marcel took the 1:22 out of Paris bound for Balbec.

That's what director Walter Asmus is talking about—
hours and hours of silence he might have in his next
Godot. The misery in the music, he said. No belly laughs
for Walter. Pain, discomfort.

Marcel got drunk on the train on the beer and brandy
recommended by his doctor. Those were the days. . . .
Even his grandmother, with whom he was traveling,
approved, fearing for his nervous condition.

But in the space around ourselves, once to
smithereens, therefrom the same silences, therein the
same eternity? A question. What becomes of Being
in unbecoming? What is sensed in the moment of
detonation, the exothermic, supersonic acceleration
of matter and memory? The Self Express, an instant
of everywhere, transcending, through heat-release,
its own objecthood. A familiar terror, yes, recalled in
our bones, we were there on entry, at the start, before

the words, before the light, really, at the instant of forming, imagine.

Marcel repaired to the bar car as soon as the train was under way. At the first stop, already bright with drink, he clambered back into the compartment with his grandmother, exclaiming too loudly how pleased he was to be going to Balbec, how splendidly he expected everything to go off, and how comfortable all the stewards and attendants made him feel! He wanted to travel again, soon, and he had just started. His grandmother suggested he take a nap. Instead, Marcel effused about the sun peeking in over the drawn curtain of the window and thought its light on the polished oak of the door and the cloth of the seat was like an advertisement for a life shared with nature.

But how does it read now? What to make of the gardens? That's where Watt goes after losing his mind in the house of Mr. Knott. Once he is expelled by the machinery of succession at the house of Mr. Knott, where once he displaced he is now the displaced, and Watt must leave, it is the inevitable way. Watt's room had but one window, no other. Watt ends up in what seems an asylum, others say it is an asylum, walking in its gardens, talking to Sam, Sam who may have been telling the story all along, others say it might be Sam telling the story all along, talking of gardens, pavilions, mansions, boars breaching fences. They, Sam and Watt, find a hole in the fence dividing garden from garden, they touch each other, groom each other, they dance energetically, Sam with Watt, Watt with Sam, and the sun shines bright upon them, and the wind blows wild about them. Somehow—*ping!*—they are joined by Mr. Knott, by Arthur, by Graves, hard by the house of Mr. Knott. *Boom!*

Marcel fell in love with a woman at a station stop; she was selling coffee and cream on the platform. He fell in love with the village of hers partially visible down the gorge beyond the tracks. Life would have seemed an exquisite thing, he thought, if only he had been free to spend it, hour after hour, with her, to go to the stream, to the cow, to the train with her, to her thoughts, with her, and thereby be initiated into the delights of the country. Alas, as she came toward him, the train began to leave the station. Oh, well, he then busied himself composing a ravishing picture, a single canvas, as it were, of a sun-splashed village, as he lurched from one side of the coach to the other to capture the glorious perspectives unfolding as the train made its way through the valley. Of course, Marcel, after his most certain session in the bar car, may have been reading the whole time, one never knows the precise landscape of a journey, since it all docks in the mind for inspection, textual or otherwise. Marcel managed to imagine a brief friendship with another traveler, artistic, golden-haired, who proposed to take him on his own journey but who instead bid him farewell beneath the Cathedral of Saint-Lô and set out westward toward the setting sun. Proust's Balbec is a fictional village, based on a real one, Cabourg, near the Atlantic coast at Normandy. Saint-Lô is not a fictional village, though it became quite unreal in the summer of 1944.

From Watt's single window, no other window, he could see a handsome racecourse, an oval. It could be a picture on the wall like the picture on his wall. Another picture. Or the picture on his wall could be a window, the other window. Whatever Watt sees in each vista, whether framed by a window or framed by a picture frame, he sees it no more and yet takes it with him, something of it, to perhaps tell Sam, in his words, about "the very fine view of the race-course" or the nothing yielded by the "painting, or coloured reproduction."

What is the sense of linking Saint-Lô to Balbec in this fashion? Where is the connection, between Proust and Beckett, Balbec and Saint-Lô, dare I say Paris and Dublin? Indeed, where is the sense? Perhaps I should fabricate one. Or perhaps the connection is plainly and clearly what it is—one great writer while young reading another great writer's work, skipping over no doubt many of the travelogue details of northwest France and the channels and seas, little knowing that some of the words—particularly the place-names that Proust went to such lengths to plumb and vivify—would be words and places that would enter his life with dramatic force only fifteen years later. After three years on the run from the Nazis, when the war ended, Beckett volunteered for the Irish Red Cross and spent eight months in the rubble of Saint-Lô, helping to build and provision a hospital on the edge of what he called "the capital of ruins."

When did Watt leave? Why does he give over to a "slow minute rain of tears?" Is he headed whence he came?

The American sculptor Robert Smithson, from Paterson, NJ, never went to art school or college—he was self-taught. Scholar Ann Reynolds argues in her book on Smithson for what she calls a "morphological" approach to his drawing and sculpture, morphology being a study of forms and their survival through various recontextualizations, whether spatial, temporal, or material. Smithson himself said that early on he began to understand things "relationally"—seeing, for example, "a container as a fragment" of something not located in any one place or even time or identified with one material. Reynolds's cataloguing of Smithson's personal library after his death in 1973 shows that he owned more books by or about Beckett than by or about any other author (with Nabokov a close second). I am indebted to Daniel Katz for his essay on Beckett and Smithson in *Samuel Beckett Today/Aujourd'hui*, which steered me to Ann Reynolds, and which came at a fortuitous time: I could not understand how Marcel's Balbec could lead to Beckett's Saint-Lô.

The *other* window.

The morphology of mothers and sons, or landscape and history, or the relation of the real to the imagined.

VI.

When I was in the university rooms, in Antwerp, doing
a workshop on *Ill Seen Ill Said*, the facilitators divided us
into small groups of four, seven or eight groups in all,
each group being provided with a short excerpt from
the late prose work, written when Beckett was seventy-
five. Each group's job was to divide its snippet among its
members, each person in the group taking a sentence or a
phrase, and repeating it aloud or silently, for the purpose
of exploring the phrase, understanding its possibilities,
physically, musically, semantically, before rejoining the
group and seeing to the snippet's integration into a
reconstitution and recital of the Beckett text, which each
group performed in separate parts of the room.

As Marcel is steered toward the bar car on the railway,
by family and medical staff, in order to overcome his
anxiety about leaving his mother, Beckett, arriving in
Saint-Lô having visited *his* mother in Dublin after his
years of being on the run during the war, returns, for the
Irish Red Cross, to a ravaged France, and does *not* go
back straightaway to his partner, Suzanne, his wife-to-
be, at their apartment at rue des Favorites, but instead

to a blasted landscape that had been pounded by Allied bombing for months, from June to September 1944, and Beckett does so in order to help in the recovery.

> My snippet was "At the other window" from the opening page of *Ill Seen Ill Said*—sentences seven, eight, and nine of *Ill Seen Ill Said* were given to our group on a piece of paper: "At the other window. Rigid upright on her old chair she watches for the radiant one. Her old deal spindlebacked chair." The four of us conferred.

Beckett was well suited to the task facing the Red Cross—bilingual, able to drive a vehicle, familiar with the French terrain, and possessed of deep reserves of empathy, and clearly a sense of duty, evinced by his service in the French Resistance and renewed by the chance of helping an effort originating in Ireland, which had remained neutral during the war. What is "relational" about these two experiences, Marcel's fictional one, Beckett's historical one, as both figures converged upon northwest France with perhaps similar fears and anxieties that took similar forms, or dissimilar but morphologically related ones?

> I now recall that we each were asked to choose a portion of this text with which we felt comfortable. You could choose the same phrase as another in the group, or you could all choose an overlapping phrase. In the end, we all, in our group, chose separate phrases. I chose "At the other window." A scholar in our group, a professor in Canada, chose "the radiant one." The remaining two, for whom English was not a first language, chose "rigid upright on her old chair" and "old deal spindlebacked

chair," respectively, each delighting visibly in the Anglo-Saxon clacking of his phrase. As I stood at my window, in those university rooms, and repeated, with varying emphases, my phrase, "At the other window," and my Canadian colleague lay upon the hardwood floor in spread-eagle, eyes closed, intoning softly, "the radiant one, the radiant one," and my two other colleagues standing at right angles to each other, looking, one east, one south, working through their phrases so that the spondaic "upright" from the one speaker made rough insert into the dactylic "spindlebacked" from the other, I felt very still. In the swirling world, four thousand miles from where I would be sent were I to die, here in this room among two dozen Beckett scholars, I am unmoving, yet looking out a window at a public, historic Belgian sky, itself unmoving, like a photograph. And this was a still piece we were sampling, written in French and English almost simultaneously, and finished, both of them, in January 1981.

The record does not show if Beckett had beer and brandy in Saint-Lô to help, but you can bet he savored something along those lines after years of deprivation. And although, as his biographer attests, Beckett was anxious to get back to his writing, his witnessing of such devastation and misery, homes reduced to rubble, possessions destroyed, the wards full of TB patients, he was deeply affected. And morphologically, you cannot argue that Marcel Proust and Samuel Beckett did not both respond with exalted forms of language, though Beckett did so much more tersely, with his four-line, twenty-two-word poem "Saint-Lô" —

Vire will wind in other shadows
unborn through the bright ways tremble
and the old mind ghost-forsaken
sink into its havoc.

Lawrence Harvey, in his seminal early study of Beckett's poetry, remarked upon the "brief and unadorned perfection" of "Saint-Lô" and its "harmony of easy phonetic flow appropriate to the gentle course of the meandering stream" of the river Vire, which flows through Saint-Lô on its way to the English Channel. The mysterious "shadows unborn through the bright ways" comes from where, if not the dark effluent of those who, thanks to merciless aerial bombing, will never be born, perhaps a nod here to Shelley's war-inspired lyrical drama *Hellas*, in which "shadows . . . unborn" are "cast on the mirror of the night":

The army encamped upon the Cydaris
Was roused last night by the alarm of battle,
And saw two hosts conflicting in the air, —
The shadows doubtless of the unborn time,
Cast on the mirror of the night.

I look out the window, in this still piece, not so ill seen, not so ill said, which Stan Gontarski has said marks the end of Beckett's traveling narratives and commences the final decade of "closed space stories," and wonder if I have arrived. Is this the stillness of terminus, the peace of arrival, of destination? I wonder: is this a question prompted by physically embodying a snippet of text with other people? Is this presentational theater, not representational? Am I now me and not playing me?

Beckett's response to a vanished world, with heaped masonry and damaged citizens left in shocking local evidence of civilization's collapse into violence, is exceedingly spare, his poem built as if by a language under rationing, twenty-two words in thirty syllables. Marvelous—for we must also live in another world, the more so if the one is filled with suffering and fear—is Marcel's highly aestheticized, voluble response to seeing a world of the imagination, in this case the "Balbec" of his mind, "almost Persian in style," a place until then only experienced through avid perusals of train schedules and place names, destroyed by actual experience. Having boarded his longed-for 1:22 out of Paris, and after the euphoria of alcohol wore off and his fantasies about milkmaids and the golden-haired fellow passenger who alights at Saint-Lô, Marcel is repulsed upon arriving in Balbec by the fact that the cathedral does not sit high upon "a rugged Norman cliff" above the roaring Atlantic, as he had imagined, but is twelve miles inland at the convergence of two tram lines and opposite a billiard hall.

> It felt so entirely other—new, strange, thrilling, like falling in love—that I entrusted myself to this other. And in its possession, there as I said it—the *other* window, the other *window*, while standing at another window indeed, in Antwerp—I saw it was myself in the other window, not in reflection, but in the square of beyond. The self I had been working on for two years was expanding into being, was even being born—an extension of interiority. With my book of stories now behind me, with no notice in the consumer press, I had found something or it had found

me. We had made it, through nerve-wracking queues in JFK and Schiphol, tense, jagged, jet-lagged vigils at baggage carousels waiting for our hapless little Victorinox family to wobble toward us and then all of us through narrow streets with the taxi drivers of, presumably, the new Europe, to the sanctum of our like-minded community, there to advance our work on the writer for whom nothing was more real than nothing.

Scholar Peter Boxall points to a wondrous vision sketched out by Beckett in his early, mannered, *Dream of Fair to Middling Women*, the long-abandoned and then posthumously published novel. "As the narrator puts it," writes Boxall, quoting Beckett liberally, "when gazing at the 'abstract density' of the 'night firmament,' this coming together in the dark sky of the seen and the unseen mirrors the movement of the 'mind achieving creation.' If the sky is 'seen merely,' [the narrator] thinks, it appears as 'a depthless lining of [the] hemisphere,' a 'crazy stripling of stars'; but if one is alert to the unseen that is threaded through the seen sky, the hidden orbits that pass silently through it, it becomes a figure for the 'passional intelligence' which 'tunnels, surely and blindly,' through 'the interstellar coalsacks of its firmament in genesis. . . . The inviolable criterion of poetry and music,' [the narrator] thinks, 'is figured in the demented perforations of the night colander.' The night sky contains within it the unseen, 'incommunicable' elements of poetry and music, which withhold themselves, but what are nevertheless 'there,' like an 'insistent, invisible rat, fidgeting behind the astral incoherence of the art surface.'"

"In a street detonation, windows in a building fly outward thanks to the vacuum created behind the blast," said the inspector. All air rushes into a vacuum, to vanquish, lessening itself in the process, until a steady state is reached.

"Astral incoherence of the art surface," that's Beckett at twenty-six years old. That's a young man deeply troubled by the fact that we are all of what we see and we see so little, who is keen to deduce what we don't see from what we do. Beckett would continue, for six decades, to test the limits of what it is possible to see or say or say is seen and then to see or say what can be said or seen of those limits, which toward the end, became his sole subject.

I was a steady state, co-extensive and co-existent with what I could see, immortal, for now.

The first paradise really runs him ragged.

VII.

There were many windows in Beckett's early work.

His first paradise, in his first novel, *Dream of Fair to Middling Women*, runs him ragged indeed.

> He could not help but notice the many windows—
> fenêtres—in his long summer-long slog twice through
> *À la recherche du temps perdu* in preparation for writing his
> study of Proust in 1930. Although no windows appear
> in Beckett's list of eleven "fetishes," those physical world
> phenomena that trigger "elements of communion," such
> as the madeleine, he admits that his list is not complete,
> and mentions specifically "a certain cluster of three [that
> are] specially significant."

Written in Paris in the summer of 1932, and at 80,000 words Beckett's longest work, *Dream of Fair to Middling Women* is word-drunk and naughty, rife with what Lawrence Harvey judged to be a "self-conscious verbal horseplay" that all but destroyed the work—perhaps no wonder it went unpublished in the author's lifetime. In it, we are treated to a paradise, asserted by the narrator and of course imagined by Beckett, on behalf of Belacqua Shua, the antihero of the book, who in the beginning is masturbating, soon after is seduced by a woman, only to end up, face in hands, in the rain, in Ballsbridge, about to be hustled forth by the Dublin gardai. But along the way, Belacqua strives to build his redoubt of the mind, Beckett's first paradise.

Marcel, Proust's narrator, writes Beckett, "is transported successively to Balbec, Doncières, and Combray by the twilight perceived above the curtains of his window . . . " In Moncrieff it is this, however awkward the translation:

If as I came downstairs I lived over again the evenings at Doncières, when we reached the street, in a moment the darkness, now almost total, in which the fog seemed to have put out the lamps, which one could make out, glimmering very faintly, only when close at hand, took me back to I could not say what arrival, by night, at Combray, when the streets there were still lighted only at long intervals and one felt one's way through a darkness moist, warm, consecrated, like that of a Christmas manger, just visibly starred here and there by a wick that burned no brighter than a candle. Between that year—to which I could ascribe no precise date—of my Combray life and the evenings at Rivebelle which had, an hour earlier, been reflected above my drawn curtains, what a world of differences! I felt on perceiving them an enthusiasm which might have borne fruit had I been left alone and would then have saved me the unnecessary round of many wasted years through which I was yet to pass before there was revealed to me that invisible vocation of which these volumes are the history.

It is altogether too wordy for paradise, and too physically busy, as Belacqua/Beckett cannot avoid heavily engaging the body in delivering periods of "beatitude" to the mind. Belacqua spends three months seeking to make himself captive, "as never before," somewhere south of Vienna. It involves escalading a hole he is in, a depression "scooped out of the world," thereby sheltering himself from the winds, waters, and visibility from beyond his ramparts. But it is a bustling place. Although "lapped in a beatitude of indolence," wanting nothing, he is accompanied by "the shades of the dead and the dead-born and the unborn and the never-to-be-born . . . a silent rabble, a press of much that was and was not and was to be and was never to be, a pulsing and a shifting as of a heart beating in sand." The whole thing turns into a place "dim and hushed like a sick-room, like a chapelle ardente"— a candlelit chapel where a body lies in state—"thronged with grey angels." One might more readily opt for the sanctuary of a pub.

Of course, Beckett could not have known that he, too, would waste many years—fifteen, till the summer of 1945—before his own "revelation" in his mother's little house across the road from Cooldrinagh, his childhood home. Beckett told both Jim Knowlson and Richard Ellmann about this moment of insight into his own work—that he finally understood that the darkness he had long struggled to suppress could be illuminated with the "light of understanding and the fire," as he later put it in *Krapp's Last Tape*. This scene in his mother's room— shorn of detail in Beckett's telling—is fully imagined by Jo Baker in her recent novel about Beckett, *A Country Road, a Tree*. Baker puts a window in the scene, in what is by far her best passage. She has Beckett seeing his reflection in the window of his mother's room, beyond which is the Tudor-style house *in which he was born*. He sees his darkness framed, we may conclude, against a backdrop of his boyhood, the house, the larches, the place he loved his father in. Baker's speculation is both bold and reasonable. Beckett, in his Proust essay, was alert to *"un corps incandescent,"* what Gontarski and Ackerley in *The Grove Companion* gloss as "the screen between [the narrator] Marcel's consciousness and the object it perceives," or, as Beckett has it in an earlier work of his own, "the zone of evaporation between damp and incandescence." Between himself in one place, through a window, through a darkness to another object, not darkness is perceived but incandescence, "the light of understanding and the fire."

Murphy's mind—the subject of Beckett's second novel—is a different shot at paradise. He does a sensible thing, given how overrun was the mind of Belacqua in his bunker, how ineffective the evasive maneuver. Murphy, now a Londoner rather than a footloose, absurd ladies' man, isolates himself in a garret, dedicates himself (sort of) to one woman (sort of), and straps himself to a chair in order to decommission the body. It is a more straitened paradise, surely, not yet vacant, but more scant of inhabitants. In the end, rather than driveling in the Dublin drizzle under the watchful eye of the constabulary, à la Belacqua, Murphy (no first name, as none for Malone or Molloy, men of few words) rocks in a chair to which he is tied, the body under arrest, as it were, or out of service, the mind free to roam unbidden by corporeal want or dictates. This is all laid out in the extraordinary first chapter of *Murphy*, which details the seven scarves that bind him, naked, to the rocker, in the corner of his room, "of northwest aspect," in West Brompton. Cleverly, his body is reduced to perspiring as he rocks through shadow, through light, the sweat tightening his thongs. With the rhythmic rocking, Murphy's body is given pleasure till it becomes "appeased," setting free his mind. And the life of the mind gives him more pleasure, "such pleasure that pleasure was not the word." Sadly, and in its way exposing the failure of his precautions or perhaps his resolve, the phone in his garret, for there is one, left over from the previous tenant, a harlot, for whom the phone was "useful in her prime, [and] in her decline . . . indispensable," he must answer it, so as not to alert the landlady, who would eventually come running should the "crake" and "rail" of the ringer disturb. Such is paradise in West Brompton, but a good try.

Thus commenced Beckett's decade-long "frenzy of writing," all of it in French—*Mercier et Camier, En attendant Godot* and *Malone muert* (in the same year), *Molloy, L'Innommable, Fin de partie, Textes pour rien,* as well as the central postwar texts, *La Fin, L'Expulsé, Premier Amour,* and *Le Calmant,* and his foundational essay on the Dutch painter Bram van Velde. Interestingly, the very first work of this period was a short story, titled "Suite." Beckett wrote twenty pages in English, before switching to French. In the end, the story was titled "Le Fin." In *le fin,* one could argue, was Beckett's beginning.

Other paradises follow, though sometimes the purgatorial might be more accurate. Might. . . . Watt's ordered world might give some peace, as the system under which the novel's world operates has a logic if not a rationale. Watt understands where he is in an order that is imposed from without, and it takes him from station to station, literally: one day he arrives, by rail, in a village; endures his term of service at the house of Mr. Knott, to which he walks; and returns, by foot, to the same station, presumably his life over as a character but perhaps to begin anew in some dimension. This comic masterpiece, written under extreme duress, by hand, in six notebooks while in hiding from the Nazis in occupied France, is itself a stop on the Beckett Paradise Local.

> Mallarmé dared not break the glass, *his idealized surface of beauty*, for fear of falling through eternity, and so turned his back on it. He too, looked for another window, the other window. A strong, no-nonsense glazier (with his son) lurked throughout Beckett's only three-act play, never produced.

"This time, then once more I think, then perhaps a last time, then I think it will be over, with that world too" appears on the second page of the first book in the trilogy, *Molloy*, and is almost perfectly realized by the end of book three, *The Unnamable*, but for the fact that neither this world nor "that world"—Beckett's life and the one of his imagination, respectively (presumably)— come to their foreseen end. Quite to the contrary: after 414 pages and 162,000 words, the schema has failed to arrive at "nothing more." For in the work's now famous final words—"you must go on, I can't go on, I'll go on"—Beckett discovered, and this in 1950, an aesthetic credo that secured the moral ground enabling art to continue after Auschwitz.

> Dear incomprehension, it is thanks to you I'll be myself, in the end.

In 1949, Theodor Adorno, in his essay "Cultural Criticism and Society," argued that the value of artistic activity was based upon the presupposition of intellectual progress, and that the barbarism of the Holocaust was clear disproof of that supposition, and therefore that "poetry after Auschwitz" was no longer tenable . . . till Beckett came along a year later and said we will go on, even if we can't, because we must.

VIII.

. . . windows, what haven't I imagined in the way of
windows in the course of my career, some opened on
the sea, all you could see was sea and sky, if I could put
myself in a room, that would be the end of the wordy-
gurdy, even doorless, even windowless, nothing but
the four surfaces, the six surfaces, if I could shut myself
up, it would be mine, it could be black dark, I could be
motionless and fixed, I'd find a way to explore it, I'd
listen to the echo, I'd get to know it, I'd get to remember
it, I'd be home, I'd say what it's like, in my home, instead
of any old thing . . . there's no end to me.

That trilogy.

". . . windows . . . there's no end to me . . ." is from very
near the end of *The Unnamable*, where the narrator might
as well be Samuel Beckett, because the futility expressed
with respect to a career spent imagining openings,
doors and windows, and the hypothetical turn inward,
to "if I could shut myself up" in a "black dark" and get
to know it, is exactly what Beckett did for the rest of his
writing life. No more wanderers, no more Watts taking

trains or A and C meeting on a road or Moran and son on a detective's hunt. No more expectant waiting, as if the without can deliver morsels or messages to the within. Rather, for the most part, closed spaces, lightless interiors, the entrapment of consciousness by memory, the isolated voice in a void, one single disembodied breath. Even the old woman in *Ill Seen Ill Said*, despite her two windows, is pinioned in place, trapped in what Scott Hamilton calls "an archeoastronomy," with megalithic alignments and planetary rhythms structuring the text.

What begins as an arguably pastoral pursuit—men walking on a country road toward (or from) villages, observed by our narrator from a rocky promontory, the sea to his east—evolves into a search for this observer, Molloy, by Jacques Moran, who, in coming across a shepherd, his flock (of black sheep), and a sheep dog, glimpses, for perhaps the last time in all of the Beckett world to come, a coherent, rational, purposeful community that, for a moment, he longs to be part of: "Take me with you, I will serve you faithfully," Moran wants to say but does not. In the second volume, the story centers on and is issued from Malone's room— "not a room in a hospital, or in a madhouse . . . [but] an ordinary room"—and Malone dies there, while writing of dying and telling his three stories and rendering his promised inventory before expiring in his late eighties, only to give way, in the final volume, to an unnamable creature of sorts, a single thorax, with a vacuole at either end, and one unlidded eye, a large worm with human consciousness—"it's like slime, paradise . . . urinous and warm."

Inspired by the darkness and the fire he sensed in his mother's room, Beckett brought fire to his inner landscape but in the end, it only exposed more darkness. There was no way out, so he stayed in, and murmured, a voice murmured, and there was the echo, a voice echoed, measuring the volume of the void. The darkness was coming, was always coming. You can see it, in the prose of *Malone Dies*, certain passages linked by scholar Conor Carville to Beckett's appreciation of the play of light and dark in interiors of Dutch and Flemish art. Windows often, most famously in Vermeer, but also in the work of Brouwer and ter Borch, played a spectral illumination across the homely features of domestic life, dignifying private moments of mysterious or perhaps inaccessible consciousness. Beckett must have been moved by this—he saw Dutch paintings in the early 1930s in Dublin and London, and in his 1936–37 trip to Germany.

This site—"urinous and warm"—in *The Unnamable*, is not the last paradise imagined by Beckett, but the last from which human agency, in the form of a body, has not all but vanished. Thereafter, in the plays and prose, fragmentation, disembodiment, imprisonment, mechanization, leading to a pronomial cleansing are the order, and, for all intents and purposes, the final (dis) order. Bodies, such that they are, actors in part, lack the human agencies that characterize real life, and neither represent nor stand in for an individual otherwise cavorting in the plausible world, like, say, Henry V or Christy Mahon. Rather, bodies, such that they are, actors in part, are the site of an enactment in which something only faintly recognizable to our experience occurs, something so faint and deep it is hardly ever reached or is summoned so seldom as to elicit a shock when touched, the proverbial raw nerve. There is a mouth, detached, floating in the dark, in *Not I*, and screaming; three heads atop three urns in *Play*, allowed to speak only when the spotlight is on them, trying to mount an argument; a woman half-buried in a heap of sand trying to look at the bright side, tending to her grooming while packing a handgun in *Happy Days*. Bodies, not being wholly there, have been subjected to a kind of debridement of identity, that is, the surgical (in this case theatrical) removal of foreign material and dead tissue from a wound in order to prevent infection and promote healing (arriving perhaps, at last, at the mysterious "surgical quality" that Wylie sees in Murphy).

He asked his friend Tom MacGreevy to recommend a book on Dutch painting. But in studying further the Flemish light he discovered a world of dark. He argued (to MacGreevy) that Caravaggio did not pioneer chiaroscuro, the Dutch did. Beckett saw the shadows in the sunshine, whether in Holland or Rome or Malta—or Dublin. In *Malone Dies*, in a scene out of Dutch genre painting, *Sapo remained alone by the window, the bowl of goat's milk on the table before him, forgotten. It was summer. The room was dark in spite of the door and window open on the great outer light. Through these narrow openings, far apart, the light poured, lit up a little space, then died, undiffused.* And Beckett, true to eventual playwright form, adds a character to his interior—Lambert joins Sapo at table—but it is of no help: *There they sat, the table between them, in the gloom, one speaking, the other listening, and far removed, the one from what he said, the other from what he*

172

heard, and far from each other. . . . [T]he earth shown strangely in the raking evening light, glowing in patches as if with its own fires, in the fading light. Beckett tried to bring the light, tried to bring light to the monad, and gave it his best, before working his way to the conviction that there was another place to look, at the other window or, as he told Billie, "inward."

There is nothing sentimental in the Beckett theater, where the past is foreign and dead. But the same cannot be said of the Beckett prose, in which fond or bittersweet or painful remembrances of his childhood are decidedly present, or in the letters, where expressions of love and attentive condolences abound. The four volumes of letters are where this other world—the historicized and personal world of one Samuel Barclay Beckett—is most clearly on display. Fintan O'Toole, in his review of the final volume of the letters in the *New York Review of Books*, asserts that Beckett remained a performer, even in his private letters, a bit of a disservice I think, especially when seen in the light of those expressions of support for the grieving, so supremely and carefully crafted. Beckett was a great writer writing on the occasion of our greatest loss, absence being his constant company. He cannot be faulted for his eloquence and originality.

So we have the great closed works of the 1960s and '70s, the continuation of the series, for in Beckett's mind, there was a series—when he agreed to have the incomplete and perhaps unfinished *Watt* published, he conceded that "it has its place in the series," in the development of his work. Everything had a place, as Beckett seemed to be always striving for something and was endlessly inventive in trying new approaches, building on past failures, as he would perhaps state it. As light gave way to dark and space gave way to cramped interiors, Beckett searched for something elemental, recognizable, an abstraction perhaps that made sense of itself and was co-extensive with its occasion. At times, what is visible is the substrate of presentation. These works are hermetic and beautiful—*Imagination Dead Imagine, Eh Joe, Enough, Breath, Lessness, Ping, The Lost Ones, Not I, Footfalls, Ghost Trio, Company, Rockaby, Ill Seen Ill Said*, and *Worstward Ho*, written from 1965 to 1981. I would also include, by way of honorary mention, the severest of these efforts, the ultimately abandoned "Long Observation of the Ray."

To director and friend Alan Schneider upon the death of Schneider's father:

November 19th 1963

My very dear Alan
I know your sorrow and I know that for the likes of us there is no ease for the heart to be had from words or reason and that in the very assurance of sorrow's fading there is more sorrow. So I offer you only my deeply affectionate and compassionate thoughts and wish for you only that the strange thing may never fail you, whatever it is, that gives us strength to live on and on with our wounds.

Ever
Sam

What is it to close the window and look no longer outward but inward? Is Being being inspected? Why are we not evident without?

To which Schneider responded:

I shall never be able to tell you what your letter meant to me—especially as it happened to come the day president Kennedy was killed.

Because "its dimensions are its secret & it has no communications to make," as Beckett wrote approvingly of Cézanne's landscapes.

Birth was the death of him.

IX.

Its dimensions are its secret and have no communications
to make. Beckett made this point about Cézanne's *Mont
Sainte-Victoire* paintings in a letter to MacGreevy in 1934.

Observation. Chamber. Inlet-outlet. Constant intensity.
Faintness. Cross-section. Constant length. Saltatoriality.
Extinction-occultation.

Years later, Beckett would make no secret of dimensions
and would in fact communicate them with withering
exactitude, both in the course of his prose works and
in his stage directions. Not that he didn't find the going
rough at times. His love of mathematics on occasion
proved unrequited. He goofed badly, for example, in
calculating the surface area of the "flattened cylinder" in
The Lost Ones (1970), which would have placed 200 people
and multiple ladders in a closed space no larger than an
oil barrel. What Beckett thought he was designing was an
interior space closer to the capacity of an oil storage tank,
such as those one sees near seaways and ports.

Observation. Observation. Observation. Chamber.
Chamber. Chamber. Inlet-outlet. Inlet-outlet. Inlet-

outlet. Constant intensity. Constant intensity. Constant intensity. Faintness. Faintness. Faintness. Cross-section. Cross-section. Cross-section. Constant length. Constant length. Constant length. Saltatoriality. Saltatoriality. Saltatoriality. Extinction-occultation. Extinction-occultation. Extinction-occultation.

The erroneous dimensions written into *The Lost Ones* nonetheless held a secret, and, whether consciously or not, the actor David Warrilow found it. As he worked through the real-math practicalities of staging the prose work, and Beckett's miscalculation surfaced (to be subsequently corrected in both the French and English texts), a miniaturization of the theatrical space may have occurred to Warrilow, resulting in his legendary Mabou Mines presentation of *The Lost Ones*, which featured a naked Warrilow moving half-inch-high human figures within an open cross-section of a cylinder, perhaps only a little smaller than an oil barrel. Audience members were given opera glasses with which to magnify their view of the severely miniaturized set. They sat, having been asked to remove their shoes, on a rubberized floor, consistent with Beckett's description of the interior of the cylinder: "Floor and wall are made of solid rubber or suchlike." Beckett did not authorize this 1975 production at the Theater for a New City in New York, but it was described to him. He liked what he heard, and liked Warrilow when they met three years later in Berlin. Shortly thereafter, Warrilow, according to James Knowlson, "took his courage in both hands and asked Beckett directly if he would write a play for him"—about death. *A Piece of Monologue* was the result.

Observation. Observation. Observation. Observation. Observation. Observation. Chamber. Chamber. Chamber. Chamber. Chamber. Chamber. Inlet-outlet. Inlet-outlet. Inlet-outlet. Inlet-outlet. Inlet-outlet. Inlet-outlet. Constant intensity. Constant intensity. Constant intensity. Constant intensity. Constant intensity. Constant intensity. Faintness. Faintness. Faintness. Faintness. Faintness. Faintness. Cross-section. Cross-section. Cross-section. Cross-section. Cross-section. Cross-section. Constant length. Constant length. Constant length. Constant length. Constant length. Constant length. Saltatoriality. Saltatoriality. Saltatoriality. Saltatoriality. Saltatoriality. Saltatoriality. Extinction-occultation. Extinction-occultation. Extinction-occultation. Extinction-occultation. Extinction-occultation. Extinction-occultation.

It is a badge of honor among graying members of the 1970s downtown art scene in New York to be able to say they saw the Warrilow performance on the Bowery (the theater is still there) during its two-week run. The house was only two or three dozen at capacity, but with music by Philip Glass, and direction by Mabou Mines cofounder Lee Breuer, those in the know knew to be there and were. I was not there. I was most likely making my way through the new Jack Kerouac biography in my dorm room in the Midwest, or rooting for the Mets to make a late season run. But I have since seen the one film of Warrilow's performance, and it brings me back to what Beckett said about Cézanne long ago. No dimensions, no communications, from a Cézanne landscape, even Cézanne portraits. The young Beckett ardently admired Cézanne because he had a "sense of his incommensurability not only with life of such a different order as landscape but even with life of his own order, even with life [. . .] operative in himself." In *The Lost Ones*, à la Warrilow, the landscape, or the *mise-en-scène*, is incommensurate with our understanding of self and space. It does not pretend to be a place for us.

Observation. Observation. Observation. Observation. Observation. Observation. Observation. Observation. Observation. Chamber. Chamber. Chamber. Chamber. Chamber. Chamber. Chamber. Chamber. Chamber. Inlet-outlet. Inlet-outlet. Inlet-outlet. Inlet-outlet. Inlet-outlet. Inlet-outlet. Inlet-outlet. Inlet-outlet. Inlet-outlet. Constant intensity. Constant intensity. Constant intensity. Constant intensity. Constant intensity. Constant intensity. Constant intensity. Constant intensity. Constant intensity. Faintness. Faintness. Faintness. Faintness. Faintness. Faintness. Faintness. Faintness. Faintness. Cross-section. Cross-section. Cross-section. Cross-section. Cross-section. Cross-section. Cross-section. Cross-section. Cross-section. Constant length. Constant length. Constant length. Constant length. Constant length. Constant length. Constant length. Constant length. Constant length. Saltatoriality. Saltatoriality. Saltatoriality. Saltatoriality. Saltatoriality. Saltatoriality. Saltatoriality. Saltatoriality. Saltatoriality. Extinction-occultation. Extinction-occultation. Extinction-occultation. Extinction-occultation. Extinction-occultation. Extinction-occultation. Extinction-occultation. Extinction-occultation. Extinction-occultation. Extinction-occultation.

Where we are is where we are not. A thousand little signs tell us so, relentlessly. Subject and object and what, where. The heart of Western philosophy, if it has a heart, is where subject ends and object begins—or where two subjects, each the other's object—share an ontology, if they do. Marcel in À la recherche strived to extend himself, as subject, into everything that entered him—smells, sights, sounds, loves, architectures, landscapes—and thereby recoup his own past, his own self, by colonizing the other, the object, the present. Beckett's sympathy for this approach may have been exhausted by 1930 after his summer of heavy reading of Proust, for thereafter, for many years, he strived to reject the authenticity of work that did not present images from which the self was excluded nor had access, spatially or temporally. And so a great literary revolution commenced, contrary to every literary presupposition of his time.

Observation. Observation. Observation. Observation. Observation. Observation. Chamber. Chamber. Chamber. Chamber. Chamber. Chamber. Inlet-outlet. Inlet-outlet. Inlet-outlet. Inlet-outlet. Inlet-outlet. Inlet-outlet. Constant intensity. Constant intensity. Constant intensity. Constant intensity. Constant intensity. Constant intensity. Faintness. Faintness. Faintness. Faintness. Faintness. Faintness. Cross-section. Cross-section. Cross-section. Cross-section. Cross-section. Cross-section. Constant length. Constant length. Constant length. Constant length. Constant length. Constant length. Saltatoriality. Saltatoriality. Saltatoriality. Saltatoriality. Saltatoriality. Saltatoriality. Extinction-occultation. Extinction-occultation.

Extinction-occultation. Extinction-occultation.
Extinction-occultation. Extinction-occultation.

Masterpieces concerning closed places of entrapment
in which beings circulate, concerning beings crawling to
and fro, following mysterious rhythms or unattributable
commands, developing a degenerative syntax that aimed
to end expression somewhere short of assertion, in the
land of negation, steadily issued from Beckett's practice.
What, if anything, this solved for him, is anyone's guess.
He was never able to remove beings entirely, nor was he
ever able to sanction them. In the cold, bleak expanses
of language there was always some detectable warmth,
if only a trace, in the distance, at the horizon, perhaps,
often a boy or an old woman, wavering in the chill, still at
large, strung in some contingency.

Observation. Observation. Observation. Chamber.
Chamber. Chamber. Inlet-outlet. Inlet-outlet. Inlet-
outlet. Constant intensity. Constant intensity. Constant
intensity. Faintness. Faintness. Faintness. Cross-section.
Cross-section. Cross-section. Constant length. Constant
length. Constant length. Saltatoriality. Saltatoriality.
Saltatoriality. Extinction-occultation. Extinction-
occultation. Extinction-occultation.

Even the other window had a window.

Observation. Chamber. Inlet-outlet. Constant intensity.
Faintness. Cross-section. Constant length. Saltatoriality.
Extinction-occultation.

PART THREE

What *is* at the other window? One may well ask—if there is anyone left at this point. I may be talking to myself, the theater emptied. Just as well, if indeed the case. No, not just as well, less than that.

This window.

Perhaps a kind of looking at everything. That's what Beckett meant to do in the doomed "Long Observation of the Ray," that closed sphere inside of which a shutter would open and close, emitting the ray of light that would systematically scan every inch of the sphere's inner surface, like an eye inside an eye, or the Eye of *Film* observing the Object of same, Buster Keaton, not through space but from within. In, always in, Beckett wrote at some point, never out. Through with out.

Consider imprisonment, what inmates call being "inside." Beckett was very conscious of imprisonment. Not only did he look out over his desk in his Paris apartment at the nineteenth-century hub-and-spoke Santé prison, but he dealt with real prisoners—and sympathetically— as actors of his plays, as correspondents. And of course, as he asserted on many occasions, he felt himself imprisoned in his body, and went on to imprison character after character in all manner of systems of restraint, whether a hill of dirt, at the end of a rope, in a wheelchair, among countless examples in the prose and theater. Murphy even ties *himself* up.

· · · · · ·

I have considered several schemes in my attempt to justify the foregoing and bring this chronicle to a rightful close, loose ends tied. But nothing sang. The most promising I reclaimed just this morning—it had gone out with the coffee grounds. In that it involved a dying actor imparting his wisdom to a young man resistant to but perhaps ready for enlightenment, it had possibilities, I thought, fictive, theatrical. A cliché, perhaps, but those can be welcome in a cold world. Despite my doubts—I feared that anyone who had gotten this far in the book would be displeased at something traditional and anyone who would like such a thing had long ago left—I am giving it a second chance. Let me be its lone proponent.

The dying actor—I have the late David Warrilow in mind—will share life and life-in-the-theater lessons with a young man whose past is unknown to me and therefore to the reader. I have assigned the young man to be in the older man's employ for a period of three years, and not just any years, but the very last of the actor's life.

I have titled the little set piece after the Beckett work that has emerged as my favorite, both for its sentimentality—it includes tender scenes from a Dublin boyhood—and for its aesthetic rigor, its courageous and unpretentious mix of the personal and the abstract, all devised "for company."

. . . . . .

For Company

GERALD, A young man.
DAVID, An old man.
MARGARET, A middle-aged woman, bartender.
MARIE, A nurse.
VOICE

Scene 1

A city bar, late afternoon.

GERALD: Excuse me. Anyone sitting here?

DAVID: Oh. [*Pause.*] Only my . . . shades.

GERALD: Excuse me then.

DAVID: No, not at all. I am done with *them* [*waving his hand as if in banishment*]. Join me!

GERALD: Thanks, I'm just in for a quick one. But I have to put this bag down. [*Adjusts the stool, sits.*]

DAVID: What's in the bag?

GERALD: Books, mostly.

DAVID: No bullion? Silver? Precious metals?

GERALD: Just this satchel. [*Pause.*] Oh [*to the bartender*] . . . let's see. A bottle of Bud.

DAVID: And I'll have another. I'd take three olives this time, if you please.

MARGARET: Oh, I do mean to please.

DAVID: Margaret, tell me, what do you think of . . . [*straightening his lapel*] middle-aged Irish guys?

MARGARET: I don't.

DAVID: You know, neither do I. Anymore.

[*Pause.*]

DAVID: So, what's in the bag?

GERALD: Couple of French writers. [*Rooting around in his shoulder bag.*] And this sandwich, it seems. Ham.

[*They both sip from their drinks.*]

DAVID: [*Wincing.*] Don't say that.

GERALD: What?

DAVID: Ham.

[*Long pause, sirens sound without.*]

DAVID: Les écrivains, eh? I've known a few.

GERALD: Barthes. Beckett. Blanchot.

[*Long pause.*]

DAVID: [*With his teeth removes one by one the olives from a toothpick, chews, swallows.*] Do you want to know which of the three I have met?

GERALD: [*Hesitant.*] Sure. Can't hurt.

DAVID: [*Smiling broadly as he brings his martini glass to the lip.*] All of them!

GERALD: Really.

DAVID: Paris. I spent several years there.

GERALD: Doing what?

DAVID: Theater. But it is Sam I really knew.

GERALD: My lucky day. My essay is supposed to be on Beckett and politics.

DAVID: [*Feigning anger.*] No politics today. [*Stentorian voice.*] Let Rome in Tiber melt. Kingdoms are clay, in the end. [*As before.*] I can't stomach it. I'm sick enough.

GERALD: Sorry to hear that. [*Long pause*] Did you work by any chance with Beckett, in the theater?

DAVID: Yes, young man, I did.

GERALD: *Godot?*

DAVID: *Krapp.* And a few of his lesser-known pieces. Late pieces.

GERALD: That was in Paris?

DAVID: Paris, London. Would you believe . . . Ohio. And not far from here, over on the Bowery. And the Public. That was a long time ago. . . . Would you . . . ? [*Summoning the bartender with a raised empty glass.*]

GERALD: Well . . . no, I shouldn't

DAVID: A pint of stout for the young man, no? No? Ah, well. Another Beefeater for me, then. Make it a Gibson this time . . . if you please.

MARGARET: I'm out of onions, darling.

DAVID: You have failed me [*Pause.*] Margaret, meet— may I ask your name?

GERALD: Gerald.

DAVID: Margaret, meet Gerald.

GERALD: And your name is . . . ?

DAVID: I'm David.

GERALD: Pleased to meet you.

Scene 2

Gerald, sitting on a high stool, alone, center stage.

In this fashion I met David. I would know him
intimately for the next three years, the last three
years of his life. I would become his employee—his
assistant, his nurse, his company as he battled his
disease. In the course of this friendship, I would
learn something about death and dying and
art. That is, I would learn about death and dying
and art through his experience, as recounted in
long sessions, on occasion (but with diminishing
frequency) in taverns and coffee shops, and in his
rooms on Sheridan Square, the rent-stabilized
apartment he kept with two cats and his books and
prints and memories. I endeavored in my off hours
to record his spoken thoughts, our conversations, as
best I could reconstruct them, culminating in what
you will hear. I never wrote my paper.

Dialogue is a polite way to have a conversation
with yourself, otherwise a certifiable tic, David told
me one day as we walked through Washington
Square Park, where he favored the afternoon
sunshine, wrapped in scarves, even in summer,
giving him the old comfort of the theater: he was as
if in costume.

Is it very old, I asked him, dialogue?

The Greeks, my boy, he said. Socratic. Old
enough for you?

People have been forever talking, I offer, putting
on David's very own brand of weary acceptance

of eternal truths. No end to it, I say, misquoting Vladimir, who said just the opposite. By then, I'd boned up on my Beckett, the plays particularly . . . for the sake of the job, which, for the most part, was to provide an amiable audience.

That's what you think, said David, quoting Estragon precisely, turning it to his own end. In Beckett, he went on to say, it really does never end—always a voice comes to one, even in the dark. And the voice is heard. Beckett can't shake that other, he said. He may even love the other, he said. David would look at me sadly sometimes.

[Gerald gets off stool, walks back and forth slowly on stage right.]

Sam was fond of counting, David said to me, as he counted the squirrels he could attract to our bench in the park with his bag of chestnuts. He said there were 104 squirrels in the park. Sam was fond of counting breaths, he added. Five million a year.

[Pause.]

Fifty million a decade.

[Pause.]

Three, four hundred million, you have nothing to complain of, he said.

In such fashion did our afternoons often pass.

[Returns to stool.]

At stool! [Scanning for a laugh, in vain.] Sixteen volumes contemplated at stool. That was Beckett's summer, David told me, sometime in the 1930s, I think. Reading all of Marcel Proust in French, to write an essay. I've read it, the essay, not the novel. It is both simple and . . . unfathomable. David agreed with me.

Love consumes its object, David told me. From Proust, he said. Beckett learned that from Proust.

I told him that that was very sad. In fact, I told him it was very fucking sad. Here's this guy dying of AIDS, and he tells me that love consumes its object? I could see it, running up his neck and face and forehead.

No, dear, he said, you don't get it: love wins.

You want to know another thing about love, he asked me. I must've nodded. The only hope of freedom is the negation of the will, he said, the suspension of all desire. You become a pure subject of knowing, beyond the determinations of time and space. It's Schopenhauer.

I think I said something like, "wow." And then probably, "what do you mean?"

He said: In the presence of your beloved you are free, to think about other things. Your memories. In the absence of the beloved you are imprisoned. You only think about him, or her. Nothing else. You hardly exist.

Proust? I asked. No, no, he said. Another. I can guess who he meant.

Scene 3

A bedroom—bed against one wall, floor-to-ceiling bookshelves on walls left and right of bed, window off to stage right. Night-stands either side of bed, ranked with jars, glasses with straws, and pill bottles. Circular throw rug on floor at end of bed. Two chairs to left of bed.

GERALD [*seated*]: You know Marie is coming in an hour.
DAVID [*abed*]: Marie. Marie? Marie!
GERALD: Yes, your Marie. To change you.
DAVID: Reaching your limit, Gerald?
GERALD: I don't do stomas well, David. I'm sorry.
DAVID: I don't laugh anymore. And I'm sorry.
GERALD: David?

[*Lights fade.*]

[VOICEOVER, *recorded, David.*] Yes, this is my voice, disembodied, at last. One thing that struck me, I don't know exactly when, about Beckett that is, is that the works displayed what I call the external mind. The works were not the interior mind, at all, but how the mind externalized itself amidst language and furniture and light and dark. I think he was ever striving to see the mind at work. Of course, this became endlessly fascinating—and frustrating—to him. To work with his productions, his forms, and find, here's the voice, there's the body, but what's this, what's that . . . another voice? In the dark? Another body? In the dark? Where are they from, are they part of my mind, my being? Or have I wandered out? Have they, has it, wandered in? What is in? What is out? Look at the works, I ask you. See them as extensions of mind, the mind taking its course. Only in Beckett nothing is false, if he could manage it, as he tried, no matter how simple, no matter how enriched by impoverishment the settings. He wrote more and more sparely. Till the end, still searching for the one word, were there one word, in any language, for the complex mystery of . . . Venus rising, whitening the stones.

[*Lights up, bedroom.*]

DAVID: Can you fix this straw?

GERALD [*adjusts straw*]: Marie is downstairs. I should let her up.

DAVID: You may [*drinking*]. The more the merrier.

GERALD: She makes three.

DAVID: A multitude! Now . . . a constant ray of light—

GERALD: I thought you said it blinked on and off. Shuttered.

DAVID: No, constant but intermittently *occultated.*

GERALD: Oh.

DAVID: What's that look?

GERALD: Occultated?

DAVID: As in eclipsed. The sun doesn't go out in an eclipse, does it?

GERALD: No. Come on up, Marie!

DAVID: That's right, no, something gets in the way, of the sun, but it is still there. Occultated. So! We have a story, a narrative, that is reduced to volume, light, surface. You see?

GERALD: I don't see.

DAVID: It is the monad. He did it. Sam brought a light to the monad—as in Leibniz. He is imagining the afterlife. Or *imaging* it is better.

GERALD: Not exactly heaven. [*Sounds offstage, footsteps upstairs, growing closer.*] Hi, Marie.

DAVID: Marie, we are in here!

[*Lights fade out for a minute; return, bedroom.*]

GERALD: You should eat a little. David? You should eat something. [*Pause.*] Marie's left. Do you want the news on?

DAVID: Was I hungry? Did she—

GERALD: Yes. You've had your potion.

DAVID: I reckoned, so. [*Pause.*] I am quite thin, now, aren't I?

GERALD: Too thin.

DAVID: I like the look of my . . . bones. I like the feel of them. My . . . infrastructure. Did you know, that the bones are the last thing to go?

GERALD: How cheery.

DAVID: And Patrick my dear departed in yonder urn . . . he is nothing but bone. Ash of bone. [*Pause, with resolve.*] No! I will not eat. On strike! You understand it's a time-honored practice in Ireland. He who can stand the most suffering, wins.

GERALD: I don't think you mean that, David.

DAVID: That suffering is . . . [*pondering*]? I . . . don't. I don't. I really don't think that. Thank you, Gerald.

Scene 4

Bedroom, faintest light. Lump in bedding, David alone on his back in the dark. Asleep. His voice, recorded, slowly, bemusedly, but with exhaustion evident.

When I was ten years old . . . I played the boy in *Godot*. It was a prison production. With a famous touring company . . . blessed by the playwright himself. The company, it was a Midlands tour, came to the prison in our very own town. My father . . . my father was the superintendent. The company consisted of . . . four actors . . . one of whom was also the director. Nothing else. No one else. No lighting man. No stage manager. No set designer. And no Boy. Understandably, no one in a prison population raises his hand to be a boy. I came to understand this later. I came to understand, later, that at other tour stops, a boy was found in . . . the local church group or a nearby school or a pub, a potboy. I am making this part up. I don't really know where the other boys came from. At ten, I was all boy, if rather slight and small—not one of my father's favorites. He preferred the company of real men, or his idea of real men. I mean, even his toy soldiers made the grade. He played with them at night. If play is the right word. In his study, drinking his gin and storming his . . . Thermopylae. Small lead men in lead skirts with drawn daggers brandishing shields. I would listen through the door and hear only silence . . . broken by the hollow clack of his trench lighter . . . snapping open and then the pop of the wheel striking the flint. As he inhaled, the silence hollowed even more. As if he was . . . swallowing the silence, feeding on it. [*Long pause.*] I was scared of the ball, all balls. I was scared of all balls regardless of size. I tried them all. Ducking away from those soccer balls, light but walloping. And the heavy rugby balls, like bloody sodden roasts, and then, but once, with the prettily stitched cricket ball I said enough to the master, and paid for it with my behind. Whereafter he attempted to teach me to address a teeny golf ball and I could not make contact in any sense of the word so that was too much an embarrassment . . . at Stafford Castle, in the wind. I could hear his shouts. In the wind. The only balls I did like were billiard balls, let me say that. Cool to the hand, the little groups of them . . . brightly colored, distinguished by solids and stripes, each with its own color and number, and all to one master, the creamy white cue ball. The slate-grounded green felt, the beveled, forgiving bumpers and the six holes would always, in the end, return . . . unharmed . . . what they had taken under . . . with a sound like . . . soft thunder, ending in a clack. Father wouldn't allow me near the pool table, however, which dominated his study like an indoor Panzer. "It's a man's game," he said. "You might rip the felt."

So I became the Boy in *Godot*. A messenger boy. I excelled at school, so predictable, isn't it? I'd sleep there if I could, when I could, and spend as much time as possible reading in the library till the janitors went home and locked up. Eventually, I had my own carrel, with crackers and jam and the books my father disapproved of having in his sight. The works of radicals, as he called them—shamans, rebels, fairies, beatniks, women. Communists. I also painted many pictures, developing a system that correlated . . . let's see, how did this work? Size and shape matched to colors. All big things blue, regardless of shape. All small things . . . white. Regardless of shape. All lines were yellow, I remember that! Circles . . . unless very large, or very small, were red; anything rectilinear or polygonal, unless very large [long pause]. I've lost it. But you get the idea. I hope. These little pictures my father never saw.

In the local newspaper that arrived every morning on our front porch there was nothing. Nothing but talk of local taxes and school boards, church supper menus, season guides—hunting, fishing, birding, planting, harvesting, preparing for winter—that sort of thing. And bland obits . . . that never gave the cause of death. I devoured this every morning, nonetheless, along with my Weetabix and juice. So imagine my surprise to see in the "calendar of events," between a "Calling All Pensioners" and a garden tour, the announcement that a drama troupe was coming to the prison for a performance of *Waiting for Godot*. Despite my provincial locale, I knew about the play.

I knew about that play because Mr. Beckett had just won the Nobel Prize in Literature and it was under "Art Notes" in the paper. And a BBC anchor had just the previous week poked fun at Mr. Beckett's latest play. Artistry fit for a prison setting seemed some adult perversion, to me.

It was my father, then, who came to me and said, boy, we have a bit of a showcase going on at the gaol.

He called the prison the gaol. Spelled it in the old style too, as in *The Ballad of Reading Gaol*. He preferred to see himself as a gaoler rather than a superintendent or governor, which is what he was.

"A showcase?" I asked of my gaoler. Where was mother, I wondered. Where ever was mother. "Yes," he said, "that is what I said. A showcase."

[*Lights slowly up, 10 seconds.*]

MARIE [*at side of bed*]: Mr. W. Are you awake? Nod, Mr. W, if you are. Mr. W?

DAVID [*rousing*]: Where was mother?

MARIE: Mr. W, it is okay.

DAVID [*looking up at Marie*]: A dream. A prison. A story. Marie.

Scene 5

Gerald, sitting on a high stool, alone, center stage, playing David's part when necessary.

It was time for his salt water—the thrush had bloomed again, his mouth and throat white overnight. Salt water mixed with apple cider vinegar to douse it.

He wanted gin.

This was our game.

No, David. The sugar will just feed it.

No, Gerald—it sounded more like "Harrow" as a soft "g" and hard "d" was beyond him with the infection. He tried, gamely, to argue that a complex sugar like alcohol kills. The articulation nearly killed him.

Alcohol doesn't kill, David. I had to correct him. It feeds. Here. The vinegar is nice and cold.

Two olives, please, he tried to say.

No *olibs*, I said.

'Member?

Yes. At Julius's. Your martini.

Seems so . . . he hesitated. Seems so. . . .

Get some rest now.

David was certain that Beckett wrote something about how much he loved math, and he wanted me to find it. I had to find it *for* him. He told me this one Monday morning. He was dying. We no longer walked in the park. We no longer dropped into bars or coffee shops in the afternoon. Perhaps someday I'll sit in a tavern and order a Guinness, or sit at a coffee shop in the window, near the light, for hours, as we did, on plenty of occasions, listening to the light, as he said, but I couldn't quite envision circumstances shifting to make that probable. Or necessary. Or fun. I'd have to say . . . it would be painful. I've not done it since. In retrospect, this had been hell. In a way. What had I done? Let's see. I took a job because I needed a job and didn't have one. This was because I wanted to learn something from even a menial job, if it was a menial job I was to get—a personal assistant, that's what I was, the New Menial—and talking with David, who'd had an interesting and important life, a life of his very own, on the fringes, in the theater, on the fringes, both life and career, on the fringes, nonetheless held the promise of providing me—*me!*—with very good information not readily available to others, and I'd get paid for it. I just had to do my job, a mix of the custodial, the secretarial, the filial. I could draw a line. I'd learn something, wouldn't I?

David would not let it go. For a week one spring I would arrive to find him in a bed full of Beckett books, all splayed open. He could not find his math quote. We searched—I searched for him, online searching "Beckett and maths," as he insisted, or "Beckett and mathematics." While it was an enlivening distraction for him, it grew to become a wearying one for me. I'd had enough of Beckett. What about me? I almost asked this dying man, what about me? I went to the Strand, finally, one Sunday, to look for bookseller help. The place is staffed with nerdy, intelligent people who struggle through life—or seem to by their demeanor and grooming—spending their time stocking estate libraries and reading in the stacks. One fellow directed me to the *Grove Companion to Beckett*. There, in an entry larger than any other in the entire alphabetized essays on Beckett, I found "Mathematics," all twelve pages of it. Although I was sure David had this book somewhere in his vast collection, when I presented my five-dollar used copy to him on the next Monday he was puzzled that in fact he had never seen the book. I propped him up on pillows and cleared his bedspread of papers and paperbacks and mail.

From *How It Is*, he shouted, or rather, at this stage, his final spring, croaked. "I have always loved arithmetic, it has paid me back in full."

Now I must admit, I *can* admit, I thought this trite. And my facial expression must have said so.

David looked at me with a pained expression, I mean a hurt expression—such a difference. It explained infinity to him, he said.

I had always thought that the universe that preceded us and the universe that was ahead of us—past and future, I guess, talk about trite, were things we could not, with our small minds, comprehend. Something with no beginning and no end we could see. Eternity makes no sense. All we know is beginnings and endings, births and deaths. We live for that . . . [*long pause*] . . . Then tell me, I said to David, what the fuck is infinity?

I will tell you. I will tell you, he said. There are infinite infinities, probably an infinity of them. But each is its own.

Its own what?

Set!

We are talking about set theory?

That's right, my boy. For Beckett, I believe math was a comfort. Because you could manage infinity by just thinking of . . . the set of even numbers, say. And place beside it another infinity, the odd numbers, say.

So . . .

So, you and I are both sets. We are infinite.

That's just theoretical, I tried.

A comfort nonetheless. Bring the gin over.

That's real.

I gave him my disapproving caregiver look.

Don't deny me this.

I joined him.

Scene 6

David, sitting or standing as preferred, center stage, lights so faint that he might pass unseen.

It wasn't until one of those dark, rainy, all-day rainy days in spring, when from the streets there is the noise of traffic sloshing slowly through the steady downpour and the guttural sound of rainfall falling through the storm drains and the intermittent concussion of thunder cracked by lightning somewhere over New Jersey, bringing a glint of light to the one window to the west and a half rest of silence to the room that I was able to get through to David, or did he get through to me? Perhaps the day, and I, had bored him sufficiently. I felt my mind was boring him and he looked up from his scrutiny of the bedspread. In any event, the darkness and cacophony told me to say, "I remember summer days as a kid in the country that were so blue, the sky so high, that I was worried that the world had reached perfection right then, with me not yet ten or eleven, and that it would never be as a good again. That this day was the high point of my existence. And that I did not know the reason for it. Why now? Why me? And why not always?"

David sat quietly in the dark. I had never uttered such an extended statement in all our time together. Though his head was up I could not see his eyes. He was in decline, in serious decline. I thought perhaps he'd fallen asleep. It wouldn't be the first time I'd put someone to sleep with my naive observations, just a first time for him. But he was not asleep.

"Give me your hand," he said. I got up. I offered my right hand in a "let's shake on it" fashion, but he took it in both of his, not without some effort, and clasped it. There was something teary coming on, I could tell, even as he looked away. He patty-caked my palm as if warming himself, and indeed his hands were cold. He then put my hand, levering it slowly, to his face, which was warmer than usual. One hundred and one, I'd guess.

"You're warm, David."

"This is my high point," he said, and fell asleep. And it was our high point as well.

[Pause.]

Apart from the faint sound of his breath there was no sound. As death approaches, life flees. It stays away. As someone heads toward the end, you think it will be over soon but it never is. Never over soon, I mean. Months passed with David near death. He revived one Monday in October, I remember the day clearly, a crisp day that smelled like fresh linen.

Come read to me, he whispered.

Sure, David. Read what?

Come read to me that sonnet we loved.

Which sonnet is that?

William, he said. The Bard.

"No longer mourn for me when I am dead?" That one?

No, no, he says. The other one we loved. About the beauty of marriage. "Let me not to the marriage of two minds admit impediment." You know that one?

Yes, I said, I know that one.

Read it to me, Gerald. Read it aloud.

Scene 7

Spotlight on empty stool at center of empty stage. New voice, narrative tone, from offstage.

He knows why he's here, of course. He knows why I am here. That's it, you see. This has been brought this far, whatever this is, however far, perhaps far is the wrong word, it is absolutely the wrong word, this is not about distance by any measure   did you see that, that shadow, a mouse perhaps, or a cat, an animal probably, of some sort, I am sure of it, in the wings? [*Long pause.*] Yes, distance. Not about distance. This all here, about which I am talking, and this talk itself, has happened, in space the breadth of a pin, if I'm lucky, a paperback. So why'd I bring it up? I meant to say this piece has come a long *time*, been a *long time* coming. Time we know, don't we? We all cover the same absolute time, but distance, some of us barely move through space at all, imperceptible to the eye, others, the privileged few, or the immigrant, move all over. But with time, say, Thursday last to Thursday week, as David might say, we all cover every millisecond of it and finish in a dead heat on Friday, still at full throttle, though we may have lost a few on the way, singers keep dying, and old soldiers, just as we gain new recruits, babes in swaddling bolting out of the gate abreast with the rest, that's what I am talking about, or what Gerald was talking about, and, you may have guessed this, no one knows who Gerald is, there is no Gerald. David knows this, too, that's why he doesn't care, as in the foregoing. He never once asked, Gerald, so, where do you live? Gerald, where did you go to school? Are your parents alive? Are you married? Are you well? How are you? I think he, David, knows that such questions would posit the existence of a Gerald and that there is no need for that, it would be a distraction. Gerald is nonliving, never lived, a cipher, a placeholder. David, on the other hand—what is the phrase in French, David . . . *d'autre part*?—exists. David came to life about two months ago, thirty-first of January in fact, after, I'm guessing here, three or four months' gestation. Who fathered him is he who birthed him, I say with great suspicion, especially with regard to the first term. Perhaps it is a mystery . . . I can only describe the process which, for better or worse, is what these 40,000 words are: a process that has reached here. Or that equals here. Are we glad we came? If you are still with me raise your hand. I can't see out there from here. Just as well, perhaps. I will proceed. Indeed, here it is. In truth it all began with a concern about heritage, a mad notion that I had discovered a secret about a filial connection between two artists, remember? I know that I can go to their texts, their art, the calendar, the ship manifests and prove my case, but along the way I realized that forensics and genealogy were not the point. The point was Being and finding a form for it, rather than hammering a certain Being into a certain form, or hammering a certain idea into a certain form. Enough with the rehash—no need to warm it up again, the ball game, the torture, the Arabian tale, the violence, the windows, my beloved in our kip, my father, my father's father, the Proust—it won't taste any different in reduction. I put what mattered into it and which my reading seemed to warrant, and I recognize a certain boing in it. Not much of a defense, but I haven't been charged with anything. Without doubt, "David" did appear, yes, from my research. He materialized, historical fact clinging to him like kelp. I met people who knew him, this vanished ghost of the Samuel Beckett canon.

I believe I have outlived him, the record would show, David Warrilow having died of AIDS in France in the '90s, but he lives now for me—and is in fact here with us, insisting that I press on. I know, that is not believable and you don't. I don't. But I do assert that the *fact* of him in talismanic fashion stands forth, manifesting—not representing—a disembodied poetics of the soul, wherefrom death can be appraised. In him I have lodged all that I have learned or gleaned from my engagement with the works of one Irish writer of the twentieth century, for convenience sake, nothing more. What matters most is to live, it is not the story that matters, remember? To think otherwise is to be removed from the real confounding rhythms and mysteries of living, which, themselves, can be beautiful, can be heartbreaking, horrifying, boring, and shockingly indifferent in what they convey, or withhold. The company of things, art, music, objects, as Proust wrote, and the company of voices, as Beckett did, is the all of what we have. And it just might make the end something less bitter, less inglorious, perhaps even less certain. Perhaps we'll go on.

That's why Beckett.